THE
VOICE
FROM THE
CROSS

THE
VOICE
FROM THE
CROSS

Richard Allen Bodey

<small>GENERAL EDITOR</small>

kregel
PUBLICATIONS

Grand Rapids, MI 49501

The Voice from the Cross: Classic Sermons on the Seven Words of Christ

© 1990 by Richard Allen Bodey

Published in 2000 by Kregel Publications, a division of Kregel, Inc., P.O. Box 2607, Grand Rapids, MI 49501. Kregel Publications provides trusted, biblical publications for Christian growth and service. Your comments and suggestions are valued.

For more information about Kregel Publications, visit our web site: www.kregel.com

ISBN 0-8254-2064-4

Printed in the United States of America

1 2 3 4 5 / 04 03 02 01 00

To my son and daughter-in-law

Rick and Beth

and my daughter and son-in-law

Bronlynn and Rick

Who have given more joy
than they will ever know

Contents

Preface

Some years ago I heard a preacher of considerable prominence and esteem in his denomination preach on John 3:16. He began his sermon with what at first struck me as a strange confession. He said that this was the first occasion in his many years of ministry—he was about sixty years old—that he had undertaken to preach on this "gospel in a nutshell," as Luther labeled it. He went on to explain that he never thought he had anything to say about this best-loved gospel text that had not been said by many other preachers many times before.

I should not be surprised if at least some of the contributors to this volume felt to some degree the same reluctance when invited to submit a sermon on one of our Lord's seven words from the cross. Probably more sermons have been preached on these texts than on any other passages of Scripture, including John 3:16. Year after year they are expounded in Lenten, Holy Week, and Good Friday services.

Yet Christians never tire of meditating on these words. That may be in part because no matter how often we probe them, nor how deeply, we discover that their riches are like an inexhaustible ocean. Moreover, taken together they bring into focus, sharply and vividly, the living heart of our Christian faith. Here are words by which we can confidently live and safely die. No wonder they grip and draw us to themselves like an irresistible magnet.

The editor and contributors alike send forth these messages with the hope that fellow preachers who read them will find here and there some flashes of truth that will beckon them on to fresh discoveries of their own. They likewise hope that others who read them will come to know more fully the "love of Christ which surpasses knowledge," and through that love will come to love him more dearly.

I am grateful to Back to the Bible for permission to use Warren W. Wiersbe's "Behold Thy Son! . . . Behold Thy Mother!"

To my wife, Ruth, my best and most loving sermon critic, I am indebted for wise suggestions concerning my own sermon, and also for her assistance in preparing the manuscript for publication.

RICHARD ALLEN BODEY

Contributors

Richard Allen Bodey was formerly professor of practical theology at Trinity Evangelical Divinity School, Deerfield, Illinois. He also served as the founding professor and former chairman of the department of practical theology at Reformed Theological Seminary, Jackson, Mississippi. He has written *You Can Live Without Fear of Dying;* has contributed to *Baker Encyclopedia of the Bible, The Encyclopedia of Christianity,* and *Zondervan Pictorial Bible Encyclopedia;* and has edited *Good News for All Seasons; 26 Sermons for Special Days; Inside the Sermon;* and *The Lamb of God: Previously Unpublished Sermons by Clarence Macartney.*

Lewis A. Drummond is a faculty member of Beeson Divinity School in Birmingham, Alabama. He is the former president of Southeastern Baptist Theological Seminary, Wake Forest, North Carolina. He was previously the first full professor of evangelism in Europe at Spurgeon's College and professor of evangelism at Southeastern Baptist Theological Seminary, Louisville, Kentucky. He is the author of *Love, The Greatest Thing in the World; Spurgeon: Prince of Preachers;* and the co-author with his wife, Betty, of *Women of Awakenings: The Historic Contribution of Women to Revival Movements* and *The Spiritual Woman: Ten Principles of Spirituality and the Women Who Have Lived Them.*

George C. Fuller served as president of Westminster Theological Seminary, Philadelphia, Pennsylvania. He was previously professor of practical theology at Reformed Theological Seminary, Jackson, Mississippi. He has contributed to *Good News for All Seasons: 26 Sermons for Special Days* and *Practical Theology and the Ministry of the Church 1952–84: Essays in Honor of Edmund P. Clowney.*

Herschel H. Hobbs served for many years as pastor of First Baptist Church, Oklahoma City, Oklahoma and as preacher on the International Baptist Radio Hour. His more than one hundred books include *Messages on the Resurrection, The Epistle to the Corinthians, An Exposition of the Gospel of Matthew, An Exposition of the Gospel of Luke,* and *The Cosmic Drama: An Exposition of Revelation.*

David L. Larsen is former professor and chairman of the department of practical theology at Trinity Evangelical Divinity School, Deerfield, Illinois. He was previously a pastor for thirty-two years. His numerous publications include *The Anatomy of Preaching: Identifying the Issues in Preaching Today, The Company of the Creative: A Christian Reader's Guide to Great Literature and Its Themes,* and *The Company of the Preachers: A History of Biblical Preaching from the Old Testament to the Modern Era.*

Paul S. Rees served as a pastor and radio preacher for many years. He was formerly a minister to ministers in Billy Graham Crusades in London, England; Glasgow, Scotland; Australia; and New York and the vice president and director of pastors' conferences of World Vision International. His works include *The Face of Our Lord, Men of Action in the Book of Acts,* and *Stand Up in Praise to God,* and has contributed to various sermon anthologies.

Warren W. Wiersbe is the former director of the *Back to the Bible* radio broadcast and is a popular Bible conference speaker. He has served as writer in residence at Cornerstone University, Grand Rapids, Michigan, and distinguished professor of preaching at Grand Rapids Baptist Seminary. Prior to pastoring the historic Moody Church in Chicago, he served as pastor of Calvary Baptist Church in Covington, Kentucky. He is general editor of the Kregel Classic Sermons Series and the author of more than one hundred books, including *In Praise of Plodders, Live Like a King: How to Develop a Royal Lifestyle from the Beatitudes; Run with the Winners: How to Develop a Championship Lifestyle from Hebrews 11;* and *Treasury of the World's Greatest Sermons.*

THE
VOICE
FROM THE
CROSS

Easter Prayer

Oh, let me know
The power of Thy resurrection!
    Oh, let me show
Thy risen life in clear reflection!
    Oh, let me soar
Where Thou, my Saviour Christ, art gone before!
    In mind and heart
Let me dwell always, only, where Thou art.

    Oh, let me give
Out of the gifts Thou freely givest;
    Oh, let me live
With life abundantly because Thou livest;
    Oh, make me shine
In darkest places, for Thy light is mine;
    Oh, let me be
A faithful witness for Thy truth and Thee.

    Oh, let me show
The strong reality of gospel story;
    Oh, let me go
From strength to strength, from glory unto glory;
    Oh, let me sing
For very joy, because Thou art my King;
    On, let me praise
Thy love and faithfulness through all my days.

—Frances Ridley Havergal

O word of pity, for our pardon pleading,
Breathed in the hour of loneliness and pain;
O voice, which through the ages interceding
Calls us to fellowship with God again.

O word of comfort, through the silence stealing,
As the dread act of sacrifice began;
O infinite compassion, still revealing
The infinite forgiveness won for man.

O word of hope to raise us nearer heaven,
When courage fails us and when faith is dim;
The souls for whom Christ prays to Christ are given,
To find their pardon and their joy in Him.

O Intercessor, who art ever living
To plead for dying souls that they may live,
Teach us to know our sin which needs forgiving,
Teach us to know the love which can forgive.

—Ada R. Greenaway

1

The Power of Forgiveness

Lewis A. Drummond

When they came to the place that is called The Skull, they crucified Jesus there with the criminals, one on his right and one
on his left. Then Jesus said, "Father, forgive them; for they
do not know what they are doing." (Luke 23:33–34a NRSV)

> My sin—O the bliss of this glorious thought!—
>   My sin, not in part, but the whole,
> Is nailed to the cross, and I bear it no more;
>   Praise the Lord, praise the Lord, O my soul.

This verse from an old Christian hymn profoundly expresses the tremendous power of God's forgiveness. The thought
that human sin, with all of its degradation and devastating
power to precipitate death, can be completely and unequivo-
cably obliterated is most sublime. It is sublime in the fact that
God whose nature is utter holiness can fully forgive sins and
in the fact that his forgiveness can reach to the depths of
human evil.

Forgiveness is the most glorious manifestation of the power of God's mercy and grace. It transcends finite human reason. The mere thought that one's entire sin account can be utterly eradicated is staggering. Yet it is quite clear that the forgiveness of sins strikes at the very core of human need and experience. It speaks of guilt gone, remorse removed, depression disappearing, and emptiness of life eradicated. What power there is in forgiveness! And it all comes abundantly from the gracious hand of God.

History is replete with the testimony of countless thousands, who attest to the fact that nothing in life brings more peace and harmony, unity and purpose, than the power of God's gracious forgiveness. Yet, it does not come easily, as the context of our Lord's words makes clear.

The words of the text were uttered by the Lord Jesus Christ right in the midst of agony and pain. As he hung impaled on Golgotha's cross he cried out, "Father, forgive them; for they do not know what they are doing." That cry of our Lord's forgiveness has resounded down through the eons of time, struck a responsive chord in millions of hearts, and brought peace, life, and new hope to the downtrodden in spirit. What words they are! "Father, forgive them; for they do not know what they doing." There the power of God's forgiveness is manifest in an unparalleled fashion. We can only stand in awe and amazement, reverence and wonder, as we gaze upon the crucified Christ and attempt to grasp the power of his fathomless forgiveness.

The Power of Proffered Forgiveness

Who is this One who hangs upon the tree? Who is this One who cries out in agony? Who is this One stripped, bleeding, and condemned before the waiting, watching, cynical world? The wonder of it all is, this is none other than the eternal Son of the living God.

The story begins about thirty-three years prior to the event at Calvary, in the little town of Bethlehem. It was on the Judean hillsides that the angels proclaimed, "To you is born this day in the city of David a Savior, who is the Messiah, the Lord" (Luke 2:11). Who is the Babe of Bethlehem? He is none other than God's incarnate Son, sent into the world to bring salvation, redemption, and forgiveness of sins. The historical curtain drops on this young life except for a few small glimpses. Then, at the age of thirty, he bursts on the scene like a bolt of lightning. Baptized at the hands of John the Baptist, driven into the wilderness by the Holy Spirit to be tested by Satan, emerging victoriously, he begins an itinerate ministry of teaching and preaching that lasts about three years. It is all a marvel of human biography. Never a man spoke like this. Never did anyone perform miracles like those which flowed forth from the hand of this man of Galilee. People hung on his words, imbibed of his presence, marveled at his grace, and stood in awe of his acts. He was the pure, sinless Son of the living God.

Yet Jesus was also a man. He became weary. He fell asleep in the back of a boat on a storm-tossed sea. He sat down by a well, hungry like other human beings. He *was* a human being. In the divine incarnation, God sent forth his own Son, made in the likeness of man, that he might combine in his own unified personality all there is of God and all there is of humanity. The incarnation of Jesus Christ stands as the miracle of miracles.

But this man came to die. And as Jesus hung upon Calvary's cross, the cry fell from his lips, "Father, forgive them; for they do not know not what they doing." What a manifestation of compassionate grace! Even those who drove the nails through his hands were the objects of his love and forgiving mercy. This is the man who died. Surely, here was all there is of God and all there is of humanity in beautiful union in Jesus of Nazareth. There was never a man like this who trod earth's dusty pathways soiling his feet with the cares and grime of this world to lift people out of toil and tears into fellowship with the living God.

If we are to see something of the power of God's proffered forgiveness we must understand the real meaning of

that ignoble scene when Jesus died. He was executed as a
criminal—yet as a martyr for his principles. He died giving us
a beautiful example of patient endurance in sufferings
because of one's convictions. He died to show us what it is
like to have a godly character. Surely these things warm us
and draw us to God. However, there is far more involved in
that hour when Jesus cried out in his agony. As the Bible
makes crystal clear, *he died in our place.* In the unfathomable
grace of God that goes far beyond human reason, in that
very moment of time Jesus had laid on him all of the sin,
iniquity, guilt, and rebellion of every human heart. He
reached one hand up to God and reached one hand down to
sinful, rebellious humankind and died in its place to bring the
two together. He made the atonement. He died sacrificially
in our place. His was a vicarious suffering. Our sins were
imputed to him. Jesus Christ, the great Substitute, took our
punishment, our guilt, our remorse, and the judgment of a
holy God upon himself and thus set us free. "He himself
bore our sins in his body on the cross" (1 Pet. 2:24).

Quite clearly, all this transcends limited human reason. No
one can grasp the depth of the atonement of Jesus Christ.
Yet, as the great Mediator, he paid the price that sets the cap-
tive free. Although we shall never in this life plummet the
depths of Calvary, the meaning of the cross is atonement,
sacrifice, vicarious suffering, and, finally, satisfaction. God is
satisfied with the death of his Son. What he did on that cross
completely satisfied the law and justice of a holy God. That
forensic aspect of the cross also defies understanding. It can
be described, it can be meditated upon, it can be wondered
at—but it can never be fathomed. God is satisfied with the
sacrifice of his Son to make atonement for the sins of all
humanity. That is the basic and essential meaning of the
cross. *Forgiveness does not come easy.*

Therefore, it becomes quite obvious that there is a man-
date for us in the work of Jesus Christ.

To this Suffering Servant we must bow. To this sacrificial
Lamb of God we must pledge our allegiance. To this dying
One we must humbly turn in repentance and faith and

utterly abandon ourselves to him, trust him as Lord and Savior and Forgiver of all our sins.

All of those tremendous truths are bound up in the proffered forgiveness of God through Jesus Christ. There is power. There is glory. There is God. We are forgiven. Life can never be the same again.

The Power of Personal Forgiveness

Finding meaning in life hinges on one's understanding of the centrality of the cross in the Christian experience. Yet, even a mere cursory, superficial grasp of all that is involved in the sacrifice of Jesus Christ immediately paints a picture of the power of personal forgiveness.

To appreciate fully the forgiveness of God and the power of the atonement in release from guilt in one's personal life, we must grasp something of the "exceeding sinfulness of sin," as our Puritan forebears expressed it. Why is sin such an issue? The answers are multitudinous. Sin is deadly serious because it is against the infinite majesty of the Creator God. Sin is a debt because it is an inexcusable rebellion against God. Sin is despicable because it offends God's holiness. Sin is a profound problem because it dehumanizes our experience. Sin is an issue because God condemns it with all of his holy Being. Little wonder that Jesus admonishes us to cry out, "Forgive us our sins" (Luke 11:4).

What is implied in the Spirit-inspired heart-cry for forgiveness and release from guilt? The nature of God's forgiveness is marvelous in many respects. First, to be forgiven is to have our iniquity taken away (Job 7:21). To "take away" sins is a metaphor that pictures a man carrying a heavy burden which is about to crush him. Suddenly another person comes and lifts it off. Isaiah tells us, "The LORD has laid on him (the Lord Jesus Christ) the iniquity of us all" (Isa. 53:6). Jesus takes away our burden by bearing it himself.

To be forgiven is also to have our sins covered (Ps. 85:2 KJV). This aspect of forgiveness is typified by the mercy seat that covered the ark of the covenant. It shows that God has covered all human sin through the Lord Jesus Christ.

To be forgiven is also to have our sins blotted out (Isa. 43:25). The Hebrew verb alludes to an accountant who blots out all debts once they have been paid. In a very real sense, when God forgives sins he blots out the debt of human sin with the blood of Jesus Christ.

Moreover, to be forgiven is to have God scatter our sins as a cloud (Isa. 44:22). Sin is like a cloud that imposes itself between God and our human experience. The forgiveness of sins dispels the cloud and the sunshine of God's love breaks forth as the dawn.

To be forgiven is to have God cast our sins into the depths of the farthest sea (Mic. 7:19). He buries them out of sight forever. The great Puritan Thomas Watson said that God throws our sins into the sea, not as a cork to rise again, but as lead that sinks to the bottom.

So much is implied in God's forgiveness that here we can only touch the fringes of the subject. For example, every sin deserves death, therefore, every sin desperately needs to be forgiven. Then, too, only God himself can forgive sins. Thomas Aquinas taught that with forgiveness there is always an infusion of grace, but no mere man can infuse grace. It is God alone who proffers grace in the forgiveness of sins. In the final analysis, forgiveness of sin is an act of God's marvelous, abounding, free grace. Isaiah 43:25 tells us, "I am He who blots out your transgressions for my own sake." Forgiveness is like a golden thread spun out of the heart of God's free, abounding grace. In the forgiveness of sins God remits the guilt and the penalty. He will remember our sins against us no more (Heb. 8:12). When God pardons a person his former judgment ceases: "My anger has turned from them" (Hos. 14:4).

All these wonderful truths abound in one's personal experience. This immediately thrusts several things to the fore.

First, release from guilt is conferred. Countless people are plagued with the burden of guilt. But as Pilgrim in Bunyan's great allegory discovered, when he came to the cross the heavy burden that he was carrying on his back rolled into the grave and he was set free. People spend millions trying to find some way to escape the nagging guilt that dogs their heels like the very hounds of heaven. It can be found only in the power of personal forgiveness in Jesus Christ.

Second, relationships are restored. We are made to live in relationships. That is what makes human life human. There are three essential life relationships. We are related to God by virtue of his creative act; we are his. We are also related to our fellows. The Bible tells us that God "made of one blood all nations . . . to dwell on all the face of the earth" (Acts 17:26 KJV). We are intrinsically related one to another. And we are related to ourselves. I can talk to myself. That is the wonder of God's creative gift of self-consciousness that separates us from all of his other earthly creatures. These relationships make up life.

The damnable effect of sin is that it strikes right at the heart of life's essential relationships. As a consequence, our relationship with God is bludgeoned and warped and twisted virtually beyond recognition. Thus we feel estranged from God. Our lost relationship with our fellows results in love-lessness. All the tumult, wars, animosities, hatreds, murder, and strife that plague the human family arise out of loveless-ness. And that is the fallout of relationships destroyed by the bludgeoning power of sin. Even our own relationship with ourselves is all but destroyed. We live off our nerves and feed on our fingernails. We live an uptight life, always striving, always feeling inadequate, always sensing that we are not whole persons. Oh, that sins could be forgiven and relationships restored! Sins can be forgiven. That is good news indeed.

The power of personal forgiveness strikes right at the heart of the issue and our relationship to God is restored. With guilt now gone our relationship with him is beautifully reknit. We begin to find the love of God shed abroad in our hearts by the Holy Spirit who is given to us (Rom. 5:5); we can begin to restore relationships with our fellows; and life takes on new meaning as we find acceptance. Knowing that we are children of God through faith in Jesus Christ and his atoning work on the cross, we learn to accept ourselves. We come to know who we really are. We find our personal identity as children in the family of God. Our acceptance with God is the basis of full and rich self-acceptance. Suddenly life begins to glow as relationships are restored. This is the power of personal forgiveness.

But the power of God's forgiveness not only releases us from guilt and restores our essential relationships; it also brings restoration to all of reality. God is not only the loving, gracious, forgiving Father; he is the mighty Creator of all the universe. One day all reality will be restored to God's original harmony and design (Rom. 8:19–25).

To be related to God through forgiveness is to be related to Ultimate Reality in the deepest, most profound sense of the word. Life's priorities get sorted out. We begin to recognize and understand what is real and meaningful, what matters most in life. Solutions to our most tormenting problems begin to come. Self-identity is assured. Life takes on a meaning and a purpose and a goal that is marvelous indeed. The power of personal forgiveness is a commodity so valuable that nothing on earth compares with it. All of this is accomplished by the power of God's proffered forgiveness through the life, death, and resurrection of our Lord Jesus Christ.

The Power of Presented Forgiveness

Finally, we are wise to recognize the power of presented forgiveness. One of the central and very practical applications of the cry of our Lord for forgiveness centers in the fact that he was showing us by a marvelous example that we are to present forgiveness to others.

It is quite obvious that every day is filled with offenses. We offend people and they offend us. This is what starts the spiral that can take individuals, families, societies, and entire nations down the slippery slope of decay, debauchery, and

finally destruction. But the power of presented forgiveness
reverses this downward slide.

When we realize the depths of our own sin and God's
powerful forgiveness, we must forgive others. When it breaks
in upon us how greatly we have sinned against God and how
graciously he has covered our sins by the blood of Christ,
how can we harbor an unforgiving attitude in our hearts
toward others? Jesus spoke parable after parable about this
matter. One of the most moving is his story of the unmerci-
ful steward:

> Then Peter came to Jesus and asked, "Lord, how many
> times shall I forgive my brother when he sins against me? Up
> to seven times?"
>
> Jesus answered, "I tell you, not seven times, but seventy-
> seven times.
>
> "Therefore, the kingdom of heaven is like a king who
> wanted to settle accounts with his servants. As he began the
> settlement, a man who owed him ten thousand talents was
> brought to him. Since he was not able to pay, the master
> ordered that he and his wife and his children and all that he
> had be sold to repay the debt.
>
> "The servant fell on his knees before him. 'Be patient with
> me,' he begged, 'and I will pay back everything.' The servant's
> master took pity on him, canceled the debt and let him go.
>
> "But when that servant went out, he found one of his fel-
> low servants who owed him a hundred denarii. He grabbed
> him and began to choke him. 'Pay back what you owe me!'
> he demanded.
>
> "His fellow servant fell to his knees and begged him, 'Be
> patient with me, and I will pay you back.'
>
> "But he refused. Instead, he went off and had the man
> thrown into prison until he could pay the debt. When the
> other servants saw what had happened, they were greatly dis-
> tressed and went and told their master everything that had
> happened.
>
> "Then the master called the servant in. 'You wicked ser-
> vant,' he said, 'I canceled all that debt of yours because you
> begged me to. Shouldn't you have had mercy on your fellow

servant just as I had on you?' In anger his master turned him
over to the jailers to be tortured until he should pay back all
he owed.

"This is how my heavenly Father will treat each of you
unless you forgive your brother from your heart." (Matt.
18:21–35 NIV)

We also lead others to God's forgiveness. When God has
forgiven us, our hearts go out in compassion to those who
are still sinking into the mire of sin. We are moved by their
plight. The love of Christ within us causes us to "throw out
the line" to them and share with them our experience of
God's forgiveness. It motivates us to point others to the
Savior. The gift of divine forgiveness transforms us into personal evangelists. It motivates us to share the good news of
our Lord Jesus Christ through whom alone sinners can find
forgiveness and personal vindication before God.

The most effective witness for Jesus Christ I have ever
known was M. L. O'Neal. He was not a pastor; he served the
Lord as a layperson. He was not highly educated. When he
was a boy he had to drop out of school and go to work on
the small Texas farm on which he was reared. Later in life he
moved to Fort Worth and through hard work became a
highly successful housebuilder whose business grew from a
small beginning until he had constructed thousands of
homes for people.

The fact that a poor farm boy moved to the big city and
made good is not the heart of his story, however. His most
remarkable quality lay in his ability to lead others to God's
forgiveness in Jesus Christ. He was something of a genius in
sharing his faith. Seldom does one see such an ardent passion
to win the unconverted as he had. He seized every opportu-
nity in every conceivable setting to witness for Christ. He
witnessed to waitresses in restaurants, attendants at filling sta-
tions, clerks in stores—wherever he met people. His whole
life was built around this one goal. I remember how he drove
thousands of miles to share Christ. As his pastor, I went with

him scores of times to visit homes where whole families were often brought to faith by his effective witness.

Brother O'Neal, as we affectionately called him, was not a great Bible scholar, although he faithfully read his Bible. He was anything but a theologian. His speaking ability was not outstanding. He rarely spoke publicly. He never held any important leadership position in his church. But he was so full of the Holy Spirit that just a few words from his lips could bring people under conviction of sin. He was so skillful that he rarely offended anyone. I know for a fact that he led hundreds to faith in the Lord Jesus Christ. He literally burned out his life seeking others for the Savior.

Brother O'Neal eventually became seriously ill and had to undergo an operation. As he was being prepared for surgery, he witnessed to the male nurse who was caring for him. Although he survived surgery, he died a short time later. His last intelligent conversation on earth was an attempt to win someone else to faith in Christ. What a way to go! His whole life was consumed with this one passion. One of the most difficult things I ever had to do as a pastor was to preach at his funeral. I felt as if I had lost a spiritual father as well as a brother. But as I looked over the large congregation that gathered in the church, I could see many he had won to Christ. What a triumph of God's power in forgiveness!

Few of us will ever become as effective in witnessing as Brother O'Neal. But we can all be as committed, and many of us could do far more than we are now. We are forgiven.

It is quite clear that the forgiveness of God demands that we forgive others. Jesus went so far as to say that unless we forgive others, we ourselves will never find forgiveness. Matthew 6:14–15 states, "if you forgive men when they sin against you, your heavenly Father will also forgive you. But if you do not forgive men their sins, your Father will not forgive your sins" (NIV). Forgiveness from God demands our forgiveness of others.

A pastor friend was embroiled in a church conflict. The feelings ran so deep that during a church meeting a leader of the opposition actually attacked the pastor and struck him in the face. It was a traumatic moment. Later, in a business meeting, the offending layperson asked the pastor for forgiveness for his ungodly act. The pastor replied, "You are late; you have already been forgiven."

That is the real spirit of Jesus' words. This is what heals wounds, restores relationships, and makes us like God. This is so beautifully exemplified in the words of our text: "Father, forgive them; for they know not what they do."

To find others for Christ is the culmination of the power of proffered forgiveness, the power of personal forgiveness, and the power of presented forgiveness.

It is surely evident that when Jesus cried out, "Father, forgive them; for they know not what they do," he was speaking to the very core of life. May we know what it is to share in the mighty power of Jesus Christ to forgive sins. The words of the gospel song are true:

My sin, not in part, but the whole,
Is nailed to the cross and I bear it no more.

How can we do anything less than respond as the song bids us:

Praise the Lord, praise the Lord, O my soul?

Lord, when thy Kingdom comes, remember me!"
Thus spake the dying lips to dying ears:
O faith, which in that darkest hour could see
The promised glory of the far-off years!

No kingly sign declares that glory now,
No ray of hope lights up that awful hour;
A thorny crown surrounds the bleeding brow,
The hands are stretched in weakness, not in power.

Hark! through the gloom the dying Saviour saith,
"Thou too shalt rest in Paradise today":
O words of love to answer words of faith!
O words of hope for those who live to pray!

Lord, when with dying lips my prayer is said,
Grant that in faith thy Kingdom I may see;
And, thinking on thy Cross and bleeding head,
May breathe my parting words, "Remember me."

Remember me, but not my shame or sin:
Thy cleansing Blood hath washed them all away;
Thy precious Death for me did pardon win;
Thy Blood redeemed me in that awful day.

Remember me; and, ere I pass away,
Speak thou the assuring word that sets us free,
And make thy promise to my heart, "Today
Thou too shalt rest in Paradise with me."

—Archbishop W. D. MacLagan

2

The Transformation
of a Terrorist

David L. Larsen

One of the criminals who were hanged there kept deriding
him, and saying, "Are you not the Messiah? Save yourself and
us!" But the other rebuked him, saying, "Do you not fear
God, since you are under the same sentence of condemnation? And we indeed have been condemned justly, for we are
getting what we deserve for our deeds, but this man has done
nothing wrong." Then he said, "Jesus, remember me when
you come into your kingdom." He replied, "Truly I tell you,
today you will be with me in Paradise." (Luke 23:39–43 NRSV)

Come with me to Calvary. Come back with me two thousand years to old Jerusalem. Look with me at a desolate,
dreadful skull-shaped rise outside the city wall. It is called
Calvary in Latin and Golgotha in Hebrew. Here Jesus Christ
hangs dying on a blood-soaked cross. The Romans spoke of
dying on a cross as *teterrimum et credulissimum*, the most
cruel death imaginable and the most terrible and terrifying of
all exits from this life.

Mark Twain might dismiss the crucifixion as simply a "discreditable incident on a minor planet." Enemies of the cross may sneer disparagingly at what they term "the gospel of gore" or "slaughter-house religion." But believing Christians have always seen the cross of Christ as altogether central and pivotal for the Christian faith and the gospel. Indeed, here is the very marrow of the gospel. Here is the fulfillment of Old Testament promise, the accomplishment of our redemption, and the divine empowerment for the defeat of Satan and holy living. Little wonder then that Paul asserts, "I decided to know nothing among you except Jesus Christ, and him crucified" (1 Cor. 2:2).

For Jesus it was an indescribably lonely hour as he was scorned, mocked, and rejected. Yet amid the cruel cacophony of jeers and insults, there was one who spoke for Jesus here. He provides us with one of the most extraordinary instances of faith recorded anywhere in Scripture.

There were, in fact, three men who died on Calvary that day. It was more than happenstance that Jesus was crucified between two robbers. Seven hundred years before the inspired prophet Isaiah had foreseen that he would be "numbered with the transgressors" (Isa. 53:12). And what is even more appalling, the holy Son of God is the object of the malicious jibes of both of these hardbitten criminals in the early phases of their suffering. Matthew tells us that "the bandits who were crucified with him also taunted him in the same way" (Matt. 27:44).

The ensuing scenario is luminous with divine grace and mercy. We see a sinner coming in repentance and faith to the Savior and making the commitment of his life and destiny. We see the Savior committing himself in amazing love and tenderness to the sinner.

Ruined by Sin

Our knowledge of this unfortunate man is limited to the two words which the Gospel writers employ to identify the thieves. Matthew and Mark use the word "robber," which is not to be understood as a petty thief or a kleptomaniac. The word conveys the idea of a confirmed and hardened criminal. The word which Luke uses is even stronger and means an outlaw. We are looking at first-century terrorists, possibly partners in crime or associates in a band of brigands which preyed on travelers or ravaged whole communities with their vicious and violent assaults.

In all probability this man had once been held in a loving mother's arms, but had become a social miscreant, a villain, a scoundrel, a vile wretch. Was there anyone there that day to mourn the execution of these two reprobates or to witness sympathetically their final anguish?

We are facing here the fact of human sin and guilt, the inevitable part of the human situation for all of us. Many either seek to ignore it or make vain attempts to dispose of it. The Bible says so clearly by way of universal diagnosis: "All have sinned and fall short of the glory of God"; "there is no one who is righteous, not even one" (Rom. 3:23, 10). This man when a boy did not boast, "When I grow up I am going to become a criminal so base that I'll be executed for my crimes and spend my last hours reviling the holiest and purest person this world has ever seen." He didn't aspire to that any more than do the derelicts in our rescue missions today (among whom I have found doctors, lawyers, and professors).

What happened to him is what has happened to us all. We all have a dark side. Our willfulness and our sinfulness have blasted and blighted our idealism. "The sin whose practice burns in our blood" twists and tortures us as surely as it did this thief. We breathe in sin from the very atmosphere around us but find the real culprit deep within the recesses of our own beings.

We can hear the hiss of the serpent in that little word s-i-n! At the center of "sin" is that proud, perpendicular pronoun "I"! There it is, unbent and unbowed, the assertion of self in rebellion and revolt against a holy God. "All we like sheep have gone astray; we have turned all to our own way" (Isa.

53:6). The ruination which befell the outlaw is not strange
to any one of us. It is endemic to the human race.

We're facing more here than what someone has called a
"relic in the theological jungle." This is more than the
"backward pull of an outworn good." This is more than "too
much appetite and too little digestion." Some today would
speak of sin as "righteousness in formation" or "embryonic
goodness." Some speak of it as the struggle upward. The fact
is that we like the robber are lost sinners, slaves of our sin.
And "the wages of sin is death" (Rom. 6:23).

Reviewing the Son

But now in the gracious and merciful providence of a
beneficent God, this wanton and expiring creature is afforded
a view of what we must call the greatest moment in the
moral history of the universe. He views the passion of Christ.
He witnesses the dying love of Jesus.

Had he ever heard of Jesus or seen him before catching a
glimpse of his fellow cross bearer on the Via Dolorosa?
Apparently Jesus was the first to be nailed to a cross. Did this
crazed creature, distraught because of his own desperate
prospects, mark at all the gracious mien of the holy Son of
God as he was nailed to his cross? Did he marvel for even a
moment at the silence of Jesus before his torturers? Was he at
all amazed as Jesus kept praying, "Father, forgive them?"
Instead of the customary maledictions and curses, the terrorist sees firsthand how "he was oppressed, and he was
afflicted, yet he did not open his mouth; like a lamb that is
led to the slaughter, and like a sheep that before its shearers
is silent, so he did not open his mouth" (Isa. 53:7).

A kind of preevangelism is taking place here and it is
impossible for us to gauge with any accuracy the nature of
the impressions being registered. He saw the inscription
placed on the cross of Jesus: "This is the King of the Jews"
(Luke 23:38). Could he even read it in Hebrew? This was
the only Bible he had. But surely he heard it quoted and
picked up the idea of kingly power or kingdom.

The thief hears the derision of the malevolent accusers of Jesus: "He saved others; let him save himself if he is the Messiah of God, his chosen one" (Luke 23:35). There are pieces of gospel here. Does he hear them? His fellow malefactor keeps on scoffing at Jesus, but his own lips are now quiet. He looks into the face of the Lord Jesus Christ. He is deeply moved and stirred to the core of his being. This is no evangelistic rally, no worship service, no prayer meeting. He gazes on the dying form of the crucified Savior.

Long before, John the Baptist cried out as Jesus approached him: "Here is the Lamb of God who takes away the sin of the world!" (John 1:29). We read that again the very next day "as he watched Jesus walk by, he exclaimed, 'Look, here is the Lamb of God!'" (John 1:36). This is ever the task and responsibility of the individual Christian witness and the Christian pulpit: to present "Christ crucified . . . the power of God and the wisdom of God" (1 Cor. 1:23–24). Can those to whom we preachers minister be described as those "before whose eyes Jesus Christ was publicly portrayed as crucified" (Gal. 3:1 RSV)?

No wonder Spurgeon determined that whatever his text, he must get cross-country as quickly as possible to the cross of Christ. There is a strange, winsome, drawing power in the crucified Savior (John 12:32). Once Thackery and three companions were walking out of the city of Edinburgh. Passing a quarry, they saw a wooden crane, standing out like a giant cross against the sky. Thackery pointed and murmured one word, "Calvary." Then all four, suddenly grown silent, moved ahead, pondering deeply. They had experienced again the perennial drawing power and fascination of the cross.

Repenting of Sin

"But the other rebuked him, saying, 'Do you not fear God, since you are under the same sentence of condemnation? And we indeed have been condemned justly, for we are

getting what we deserve for our deeds'" (Luke 23:40–41a).
A change of mind has taken place. There has been a turn-
around of 180 degrees. This is precisely what the Bible
speaks of as repentance.

Most ominously the call to repentance has waned in our
time. Yet repentance is mandated in both Testaments. William
Booth, founder of the Salvation Army, used to say that the
chief dangers in this century would be religion without the
Holy Spirit; Christianity without Christ; forgiveness without
repentance; politics without God; and heaven without hell.

Universalists and others play down repentance because they
believe that God has forgiven us even before we repent. Some
conservatives reject repentance for salvation out of the fear
that it might become a meritorious act. Like faith, which is a
gift of God (Eph. 2:8–9), repentance is given as a gracious
gift of God as the Spirit of God through the Word of God
interacts with the needy human heart (Acts 11:18; Rom. 2:4).
"Repentance toward God and . . . faith toward our Lord
Jesus" (Acts 20:21) are flip sides of the same coin. This was
the message of Paul, and it must be our message, too.

How can people trust in Christ as Savior from sin without
acknowledging the fact of their own heinous sin and turning
from it? Christ and the apostles preached repentance, for
indeed God "commands all people everywhere to repent"
(Acts 17:30). The publican cried, "God, be merciful to me, a
sinner!" (Luke 18:13). Paul said to the Philippian jailer,
"Believe on the Lord Jesus, and you will be saved" (Acts
16:31). He did not need to mention repentance because the
poor fellow was totally wiped out and almost over the edge.

We have to confess: our problem is more than our com-
plexes and poor adjustment to our environment. One modern man said, "I have nothing to confess. I have not sinned. I
am clear with God. I did nothing wrong. I have no regrets."
His name was Adolph Eichmann, the Nazi butcher.

True repentance involves a turning from sin and a willing-
ness to confess and forsake it. The prodigal's repentance
involved more than getting sick of the pig pen and saying, "I
will get up and go to my father" (Luke 15:18). It required his

rising up and going to his father. John the Baptist insisted, "Produce fruit in keeping with repentance" (Matt. 3:8 NIV).

This is what we see so vividly and graphically in the outlaw. He breaks clearly and decisively with the old pattern of life. He renounces all participation in the profane harangues of which he had a part. With the help of the Spirit of God, he is heading in a new direction.

Recognizing the Savior

A vital and saving faith must have as its proper object the Lord himself. Somehow this agonized soul sees through the mockery and the misery of the experience in which he is so painfully embroiled and recognizes Christ as a King about to possess a kingdom. He keeps saying, "Remember me, remember me" (Luke 23:42).

What does this imply concerning his understanding of who Jesus is? After all, the absolutely crucial question is, "Who is this?" (Matt. 21:10). It is the issue Jesus broached to his disciples: "Who do people say that the Son of Man is?" (Matt. 16:13). Here is where the historic heresies and the cults go astray. The identification of Jesus Christ goes to the very heart of what Christianity really is.

The theological grasp of the terrorist was admittedly very limited. How much does one need to understand about Christ in order to be saved? The heat generated by the lordship/salvation issue in our time indicates how germane this question is. I think it was the late E. Stanley Jones who said, "God expects us to give as much of ourselves as we can to as much of Christ as we understand." The depth and comprehensiveness of our spiritual commitment will be determined by many factors, including age, background, and circumstances. But we would be making a serious blunder if we did not allow a sovereign God to respond to the faintest cry in the last moment of life. For it is a God of mercy who says, "everyone who calls on the name of the Lord shall be saved" (Rom. 10:13).

The terrorist with all of his limitations affirms the utter uniqueness and sinlessness of Jesus Christ. He does not seem to put Jesus in a simply human category. He expresses belief in an existence beyond this life. As the looming horror of the shades settles upon him, the robber realizes he needs a mediator, one who can put in a word for him. His sin and guilt will require someone to remember him, and he casts himself and his destiny into the crucified hands of Jesus Christ. What rich opportunities we have had by contrast. Do we truly believe?

Receiving Salvation

"And he said to him, 'Truly I tell you, today you will be with me in Paradise'" (Luke 23:43). The reply of the Lord Jesus is certain and final, clear and unequivocal. Surely he has "the words of eternal life" (John 6:68). Here speaks the sinless and spotless Lamb of God. Here speaks the sin bearer, the substitute. He is on the cross in an altogether unique capacity. He is dying as "the just for the unjust, that he might bring us to God" (1 Pet. 3:18 KJV). Little did the terrorist realize the transaction that was taking place right then, as indeed little does any of us realize the enormity and thoroughness of the work accomplished by Christ on the cross.

The truth is that if Christ is not our substitute, we are still under condemnation. If our sin and guilt have not been transferred to him, they are still on us and we are goners.

The answer of Jesus was a prophecy. His was not to be a long, lingering death as he languished on his cross for perhaps even several days, a not uncommon ordeal. Jesus says, "Today." Likewise the passage of the transformed terrorist into eternal bliss is not to be an elongated struggle or a prolonged epoch of unconsciousness.

The answer of Jesus is also a promise. "You will be with me." The Savior always does infinitely more for us than we can ask or think. The bandit had pleaded, "Remember me."

He is given the glorious promise, "You will be with me." "In your presence there is fullness of joy" (Ps. 16:11).

The answer of Jesus is also a provision. "In Paradise." No maybe, could be, hope so. The bankrupt sinner is given life eternal. "The free gift of God is eternal life in Christ Jesus our Lord" (Rom. 6:23).

> There was no other good enough
>   To pay the price of sin,
> He only could unlock the gate
>   Of heaven and let us in.

What a magnificent paradigm of God's gracious and eternal salvation for us lost sinners! What clarification is lent to our understanding of a right relationship to the Father through the Son! Here is a clear repudiation of any sacramentalism. No room for any doctrine of purgatory here. No room for any wistful universalism here. The terrorist came, as every one of us must come, to find the cross of Christ the touchstone of our eternal destiny.

We sing it with joy:

> The dying thief rejoiced to see
> That fountain in his day;
> And there may I, though vile as he,
> Wash all my sins away.

But one solemn shadow remains. An old preacher once warned against procrastination in the matter of seeking the Lord's salvation. His burden was that his hearers should not delay or wait, thinking to receive Christ at the last moment of life. A raucous challenger shouted out, "But what about the thief on the cross?" The minister replied, "Oh yes, but which thief?" This is the issue we must face.

Redemption

Having been tenant long to a rich lord,
    Not thriving, I resolved to be bold
    And make a suit unto him, to afford
A new small-rented lease, and cancel the old.

In heaven at his manor I him sought;
    They told me there that he was lately gone
    About some land, which he had dearly bought
Long since on earth, to take possession.

I straight returned, and knowing his great birth,
    Sought him accordingly in great resorts;
    In cities, theaters, gardens, parks, and courts;
At length I heard a ragged noise and mirth
    Of thieves and murderers; there I him espied,
    Who straight, *Your suit is granted,* said, and died.

—George Herbert

Jesus, loving to the end
Her whose heart thy sorrows rend,
And thy dearest human friend:
Hear us, holy Jesus.

May we in thy sorrows share,
For thy sake all peril dare,
And enjoy thy tender care:
Hear us, holy Jesus.

May we all thy loved ones be,
All one holy family,
Loving for the love of thee:
Hear us, holy Jesus.

—Thomas Benson Pollock

3

Behold Thy Son! . . .
Behold Thy Mother!

Warren W. Wiersbe

When Jesus therefore saw his mother, and the disciple standing by, whom he loved, he saith unto his mother, "Woman,
behold thy son!" Then saith he to the disciple, "Behold thy
mother!" (John 19:26–27 KJV)

If you and I had been in Jerusalem that passover afternoon
when Jesus was crucified, I wonder how near the cross we
would have stood. It is one thing to sing, "Jesus, keep me
near the cross"; it is quite another thing to actually stay
there. The Roman soldiers were there, but only out of duty.
Three women and John were there; but they were not there
because of duty. They were there out of devotion; they loved
the Lord Jesus. Mary, his mother, was there; Mary
Magdalene was there; Salome, his mother's sister, was there;
and John was there.

We use the phrase "near the cross" quite often. It has

43

become one of our evangelical clichés. We've prayed, "O Lord, keep me near the cross," and we sing about standing near the cross. What does it really mean to be near the cross of Jesus?

Obviously, we are not talking about literal geography. The cross is gone, and you and I are not able to go outside the city wall of Jerusalem and stand near the cross. We are talking about a spiritual position; we are talking about a special relationship to Jesus Christ.

This third word from the cross helps us to understand what it means to be near the cross. Perhaps the best thing we can do is talk to the people who were there. Let's interview Mary Magdalene, Salome, Mary, and John to find out what it really means to be near the cross of Jesus Christ. What did the cross mean to each of these persons?

A Place of Redemption

Let's begin with Mary Magdalene. She is listed last in John 19:25, but I want to start with her. If you had walked up to Mary Magdalene that afternoon and said, "Mary Magdalene, you are standing near the cross. What does it mean to you?" I think she would have answered, "The cross to me is a place of redemption."

Mary Magdalene had been delivered by the Lord Jesus Christ. It is unfortunate that some Bible students and preachers have confused the woman in Luke 7 with Mary Magdalene. Luke 7:36–50 records an event in which our Lord was having dinner with a Pharisee when a woman of the streets came in—a woman of very unsavory reputation. She worshiped the Lord Jesus and anointed him with expensive perfume. Many people have identified this woman as Mary Magdalene, but this is not true. We do not know this woman's name.

Mary Magdalene is mentioned in Luke 8:2 as a woman out of whom Jesus had cast seven demons. (This same fact is recorded in Mark 16:9.) Mary Magdalene had been in bondage to Satan. I personally cannot conceive of what it would be like to be possessed by one demon, let alone seven! We do not know what they made her do, but she was in terrible bondage. Now before we judge her, let's remember that Ephesians 2:1–3 makes it very clear that every unsaved person is walking "according to the prince of the power of the air, the spirit that now worketh in the children of disobedience." Demonic forces are at work in the lives of unbelievers today, and these demonic forces would like to oppress the minds and distress the hearts of God's people as well. Satan was at work in Mary Magdalene's life until Jesus delivered her from those demonic powers.

Whenever I think of deliverance, I think of Acts 26:18. God spoke these words to Paul to tell him what his ministry of the gospel was going to be: "To open their eyes, and to turn them from darkness to light, and from the power of Satan unto God, that they may receive forgiveness of sins, and inheritance among them which are sanctified by faith that is in me." When you trust the Lord Jesus Christ, these marvelous changes take place in your life. You go from darkness to light—from mental darkness, moral darkness, and spiritual darkness into the wonderful light of the gospel of Jesus Christ. You go from the power of Satan to the power of God. God begins to control and to use you. You go from guilt to forgiveness, and from poverty to wealth as an heir of God through faith in Jesus Christ. This is what Jesus did for Mary Magdalene.

This miracle of redemption is a costly thing. When Jesus delivered Mary Magdalene from the power of the wicked one, it cost him something. Standing there at the cross, Mary saw the price being paid. You see, Jesus had to die that we might be redeemed. For me to move out of the darkness into the light, he had to move from the light into the darkness. For me to be delivered from Satan to God, Jesus Christ had to be forsaken by God. For me to be delivered from guilt to forgiveness, Jesus had to be made sin for me. For him to make me rich, he had to become the poorest of the poor. No wonder Mary was standing there at the cross. No wonder she was there when Jesus was buried. No wonder she came to the tomb early on resurrection morning. Mary Magdalene had experienced redemption. Standing near the cross, Mary said, "The cross to me is a place of redemption."

Is the cross a place of redemption in your life? Can you say, "I have trusted Jesus Christ, and he has moved me from darkness to light, from the power of Satan to the power of God, from the guilt of sin to forgiveness, from poverty to an inheritance through faith in him?" If this is not true in your life, then you are missing all that Jesus died to give you. Ask him to save you, and then you can take your stand near the cross, a place of redemption.

A Place of Rebuke

The second person I'd like us to talk to is Salome. Salome was an interesting person. She was Mary's sister, the mother of James and John, and the wife of Zebedee. We remember her as the woman who came to Jesus asking that her sons might sit on thrones. In Matthew 20:20–28 we have the account. Salome and James and John came to Jesus and said, "We want to ask something of you." Jesus said, "What do you want?" They had heard him say that the apostles were going to judge the twelve tribes of Israel, that they were going to sit on thrones—and they wanted to be sure they had good seats! They said to Jesus, "We would like to have the thrones on your right hand and on your left." Jesus said, "Are you able to drink the cup I'm going to drink? Are you able to be baptized with the baptism I'm going to experience?" Very glibly they said, "Yes we are." He said, "You will; indeed, you will." James was the first of the apostles to be martyred; John was the last of the apostles to die, but he went through great persecution and suffering before he was called home.

"Salome, we want to ask you, what kind of a place is the cross? You are standing near the cross. What does it mean to you?" I think she would have answered, "The cross to me is a place of rebuke. I stand here rebuked, because I was so self-ish. I wanted my two sons to have the places of honor. I wanted them at the right hand and the left hand of the Lord Jesus Christ; now I stand here seeing him not on a throne but on a cross, and I'm ashamed of myself."

Indeed, she might well be ashamed of herself—as all of us should be when we pray selfishly! Her prayer was a selfish prayer. "I want something for my sons; I don't care what it costs. I want it!" Her prayer was born of pride, not of humil-ity. Did these two men deserve thrones? Thrones are not given carelessly; they must be earned. Salome had forgotten the cost of true reward. There is no crown without a cross; there is no wearing of the crown without the drinking of the cup. Even our Lord Jesus Christ himself did not return to the throne except by way of the cross.

The cross to Salome was a place of rebuke. How much we need to sing,

> When I survey the wondrous cross
> On which the Prince of Glory died,
> My richest gain I count but loss,
> And pour contempt on all my pride.
>
> Forbid, it, Lord, that I should boast,
> Save in the death of Christ my God:
> All the vain things that charm me most,
> I sacrifice them to His blood.

Sometimes the most selfish things that we do come because of our wrong praying. Christians do not rise any higher than their prayers. Salome did not bring her prayers to the cross. As a consequence, her praying was selfish, earthly, proud, and ignorant. She did not realize the price she was going to pay.

God will answer prayer, but we must be sure we can pay the price. James paid a price—he was martyred. John paid a price—he had to suffer and was persecuted. Salome looked upon the cross as a place of rebuke, and I confess to you that many times as I have contemplated the cross I have been rebuked, because my praying has been selfish, my praying has been proud. God has looked upon me and said, "Are you willing to drink the cup?" "Oh no, Lord, I want the answer to prayer." "But you must drink the cup. Are you willing to be baptized with the baptism of suffering?" "No, God, I just want the blessing, not the suffering!" Salome says to each of us, "The cross is a place of rebuke."

God delights in honoring his servants and his people. One day we are going to share in his eternal glory. But before the glory there has to be the suffering: "The God of all grace, who hath called us unto his eternal glory by Christ Jesus, after that ye have suffered a while" (1 Pet. 5:10). Mary Magdalene told us that the cross is a place of redemption. Have you been redeemed? Salome told us that the cross is a place of rebuke. Perhaps as we stand near the cross, God rebukes our selfishness, pride, and desire for glory without suffering.

A Place of Reward

Now we want to look at Mary, the mother of our Lord Jesus. If you had stood by Mary at Calvary and asked her, "What does it mean for you to be near the cross?" I think she would have replied, "The cross to me is a place of reward."

It is interesting to note that we find Mary at the beginning of the Gospel of John (chap. 2) and at the end of the Gospel of John (chap. 19). In John 2, Mary is experiencing the joys of a wedding feast. In John 19 she is experiencing the sorrows of a funeral. In John 2 the Lord Jesus Christ displays his power. He manifests his glory and turns water into wine. But in John 19 our Lord Jesus Christ dies in weakness and in shame. He could have exercised his power and delivered himself, but had he done so, he would not have completed the work of salvation. He did not come to save himself; he came to save us.

In John 2 we find Mary speaking, but in John 19 Mary is

silent. Her silence is significant. We expect her to say something in John 2. The host had run out of wine. This was a
social disgrace back in Jesus' day. In fact, I read somewhere
that a person could be fined for inviting people to a feast and
not having sufficient wine. Mary came to Jesus and said,
"They have no wine." He met the need out of his gracious
heart of love.

In John 19, Mary is silent. I believe the one person who
could have rescued Jesus from the cross was his mother,
Mary! All Mary would have had to do was to walk up to
those Roman soldiers and say, "I am his mother; I understand him better than anyone else. What he says is not true;
therefore, would you deliver him?" Had Mary given this kind
of witness, she could have saved the Lord Jesus, but she kept
quiet. Do you know why she kept quiet? She could not lie.
As she stood there by the cross, her silence was testimony
that Jesus Christ is the Son of God. If anybody knows a son,
certainly it is his mother. If Jesus Christ were not what he
claimed to be, Mary could have saved him. She kept silent,
and her silence is an eloquent testimony that the Jesus Christ
we worship is God, God the Son come in human flesh.

The cross was a place of reward for Mary in the sense that
the Lord Jesus Christ did not ignore her but rewarded her by
sharing his beloved disciple with her. Mary is to be honored,
but she is not to be worshiped. We are told in the Gospel of
Luke that Mary herself said she rejoiced in God her Savior
(Luke 1:47). Mary was saved by faith like any other sinner.
Elizabeth did not say to her, "Blessed art thou *above*
women," but "Blessed art thou *among* women" (v. 42). We
do bless Mary, because she suffered in order to bring the
Savior into the world.

Simeon had said to her, "A sword shall pierce through thy
own soul also" (Luke 2:35). She experienced the climax of
that suffering at the cross. When she was discovered to be
with child, she began to suffer shame and reproach. She was
misunderstood. People gossiped about her. She was married
to Joseph, a poor carpenter, and lived in poverty. She gave
birth to the Lord Jesus in a lowly stable. Then they had to

flee from Bethlehem to escape the sword; some innocent children died because of her baby. I wonder how Mary felt about that. She rejoiced that her child was delivered, but she must have felt the sword in her own soul when she heard that other innocent children had died.

When our Lord Jesus was a youth, he said to her, "Wist ye not that I must be about my Father's business?" (Luke 2:49). Thus began a process of separation, a growing separation. At times Mary did not really understand him. The sword was going through her own soul! The psalmist expresses it so eloquently: "I am become a stranger unto my brethren, and an alien unto my mother's children" (Ps. 69:8). The sword was going through Mary's soul.

At the cross, Mary experienced the climax of that suffering. She suffered because he died. She suffered because of the way he died—on a cross, numbered with the transgressors. She suffered because of where he died—in public, with all sorts of people going by. It was such a cosmopolitan crowd that Pilate wrote the declaration for the cross in three different languages! Our Lord was not crucified in a corner somewhere. Openly, publicly, shamefully he was crucified. And there Mary stood, feeling the sword go through her soul.

But Jesus saw her, and Jesus assured her of his love. He always does this. You may be going through a Calvary experience. You may be standing by and suffering intensely because of something that has happened. I want you to know that the Lord Jesus Christ always assures us of his love. He said to her, "Woman (a title of respect), behold thy son!" Was he speaking about himself? I don't think so; I think he was talking about John. Then he said to John, "Behold thy mother!" What was he doing? He was establishing a new relationship. He was saying to Mary, "I am going to go back to heaven. Because of this, you and I must have a whole new relationship. But in order to give peace to your heart, in order to heal your broken heart where the sword has pierced so deeply, I'm giving you John." He assured her of his love as he took his choice disciple and made him Mary's son. The

Lord Jesus felt her sorrow, he knew her loneliness, and he rewarded her by giving to her the disciple whom he loved so dearly.

I read somewhere that the longest will ever probated was made up of four big volumes. There were 95,940 words in it! The shortest will on record is recorded in Great Britain, and it has only three words to it: "All for mother."

Jesus did not have any earthly possessions to give to any-body. The soldiers had gambled for his clothes and had taken them away. What could he give to Mary? He gave John to Mary. From that very hour John took her into his own house (John 19:27). To Mary the cross was a place of reward. Ultimately God rewards those who have suffered.

A Place of Responsibility

And now we must speak to John, the disciple whom Jesus loved. "John, what does it mean to you to be near the cross?" I think John would answer, "It is a place of responsi-bility." Our Lord Jesus reigned from the cross. He was in control. He was giving the orders. He was directing his own followers and his loved ones. He restored John. John had forsaken him and fled. All the disciples had done this. The Shepherd had been smitten, and the sheep had scattered. But John came back to the cross. And he was restored and for-given!

You and I may stray, we may disobey, we may even deny our Lord, but we can come back. John came back to the cross. That was not the safest or easiest place to stand. I have watched people die, but not in that kind of a situation. It took courage and love for John to come back. The Lord Jesus restored John, and it was John who one day wrote: "If we confess our sins, he is faithful and just to forgive us our sins, and to cleanse us from all unrighteousness" (1 John 1:9).

Jesus not only restored John, but also honored him. He said, "John, I am no longer going to be on earth to watch over my earthly mother, Mary, so you are going to take my place. You are going to take my mother, and you are going to be a son to her."

The interesting thing is this: all of us are taking his place! He said, following his resurrection, "As My Father hath sent me, even so send I you" (John 20:21). You and I represent Jesus Christ to others. John was to love Mary, because he would be taking our Lord's place in Mary's life. You and I are to love others the way the Lord Jesus has loved us. John was the disciple whom Jesus loved, and John was the disciple who loved the Lord Jesus. It is interesting to note in the latter chapters of the Gospel of John how John showed his love for the Lord Jesus.

In John 13:23 we read that John leaned on Jesus' breast, learned his secrets. Love is always close to the heart. In John 19:26 we learn that John stood at the cross. It is one thing to lean on Jesus' breast privately in the upper room, but it is quite something else to stand publicly by the cross. But love always stands and suffers. John 20:4 tells us that John ran to the tomb. He recognized Jesus and said, "It is the Lord!" (John 21:7). Love always recognizes the beloved one. Then love followed (vv. 19–20). Jesus said, "Follow me," and John began to follow the Lord Jesus. Finally, love testified (v. 24). John said, "I am testifying of these things—I saw them; I know that they are true."

The cross is a place of responsibility. If you and I have come to the cross, we have a big responsibility—the responsibility of loving the Lord Jesus and then living for the Lord Jesus and loving others. The Christian life is not an easy life, but it is a wonderful life. I believe the Christian life is a lot easier than a sinful life! "Near the cross"—that's where he wants us to be. "Near the cross" is a place of redemption. If you have never trusted the Lord Jesus, you can be redeemed. Just come to the cross in faith and trust him. "Near the cross" is a place of rebuke. All of our pride and selfishness fade away as we stand at the cross and see the Lord Jesus suffering for us. "Near the cross" is a place of reward. "Woman, behold thy son! . . . Behold thy mother!" "Near the cross" is a place of responsibility. When we come to the cross through faith in Jesus Christ, we cannot run away, we cannot hide. We must stand there, identified with him in the fellowship of his sufferings. Then we must go to do the work he has called us to do.

Whatever God has called you to do, my friend, do it. If you will come near the cross, you will discover what a wonderful place it really is!

Redemption

A Mother and her Child;
   A wondrous boy,
A dead man raised to life;
A few poor fishermen,
An Upper Room,
A feast, a garden, and a judgment hall.

A crown of thorns, a scourge,
   A bitter Cross;
A great stone rolled away
   And tears;
A springtime morning
And an empty tomb;
A Feast, a Blessing, and a Risen Christ.

               —Mary Winter Ware

Throned upon the awful tree,
King of grief, I watch with thee.
Darkness veils thine anguished face:
None its lines of woe can trace:
None can tell what pangs unknown
Hold thee silent and alone.

Silent through those three dread hours,
Wrestling with the evil pow'rs,
Left alone with human sin,
Gloom around thee and within,
Till th' appointed time is nigh,
Till the Lamb of God may die.

Hark, that cry that peals aloud
Upward through the whelming cloud!
Thou, the Father's only Son,
Thou, his own Anointed One,
Thou dost ask him—can it be?
"Why hast Thou forsaken Me?"

Lord, should fear and anguish roll
Darkly o'er my sinful soul,
Thou, who once was thus bereft
That thine own might ne'er be left,
Teach me by that bitter cry
In the gloom to know thee nigh.

—John Ellerton

4

A Window on Hell

Richard Allen Bodey

"My God, my God, why have you forsaken me?" (Matt. 27:46 NRSV)

Martin Luther once sat motionless for hours, as if in a trance. Denying himself food and drink, he remained absorbed in deep contemplation. Finally, he stood up and exclaimed, "God forsaken by God! Who can understand that?"

The Bible has its corridors of mystery which refuse to yield their secrets to anyone, even the most brilliant theologians. But nowhere in all the Bible do we encounter any mystery that so staggers the mind and shocks the Christian consciousness as this tortured cry from the lips of our dying Savior, "My God, my God, why have you forsaken me?" Indeed, so shocking, so incredible to some is the thought that Jesus should have spoken like this that they doubt, even deny, that the words were really his. They are, of course, greatly mistaken. This awesome, haunting protest screamed into the

57

darkened heavens brings us to the heart of the atonement. Here is the "crucifixion within the crucifixion."

Although the full significance of these words will forever elude us, they nevertheless have much of momentous importance to teach us. We shall view them from several angles.

The Words from Jesus' Perspective

Many interpreters who acknowledge that Jesus spoke these words tone them down. They remind us that he was quoting from the opening verse of Psalm 22. He was identifying with the experience of the psalmist in one of the psalmist's most bitter hours of spiritual anguish and despair. They argue that our Lord's desolation was wholly internal and subjective. It belonged only to his own inner world of feeling and perception. Overwhelmed by the excruciating pain of crucifixion and the long hours of cruel abuse preceding it, crushed by the weight of human sin so repulsive to his sinless soul, he felt forsaken by God. He lost all consciousness of his Father's love and fellowship. He was like a person groping in the dark for a light, unable to find it, although it is there all the while. It seemed to Jesus that God had abandoned him, but nothing could be further from the truth.

Said one eminent preacher confidently, "We know that in that awful moment Jesus was not really forsaken." Others even assert that God was never closer to Jesus than during those three hours of darkness and agony, when Jesus groped for him but could not find him.

If this is true, whatever he may have suffered on Calvary, our Lord did not suffer the full penalty for sin. God is holy. He cannot tolerate sin. He cannot stomach even the sight of it. "Your eyes are too pure to behold evil, and you cannot look on wrongdoing," cried the prophet Habakkuk (Hab. 1:13). In his purity God recoils from sin. He banishes sinners from his presence. So Adam and Eve were expelled from Eden, the place of perfect communion with God. So in his vision of heaven John saw that nothing sinful or unclean can ever pass through its gates.

Now the very heart of the Christian faith is the fact that on the cross Jesus took our sins upon himself. "For our sake," writes Paul, "(God) made him to be sin who knew no sin" (2 Cor. 5:21). Paul does not say that Jesus *became a sinner*, he says that Jesus *became sin*. He became, in effect, the incarnation of every hideous shape of sin and wickedness ever conceived. A pastor I know put it graphically by saying that Jesus became a "hunk of sin."

Peter tells us that "he himself bore our sins in his body on the cross" (1 Pet. 2:24). In biblical terms, to bear sin means to suffer the penalty for sin. This is precisely what Jesus did on the cross. Paul says that he became a curse for us (Gal. 3:13). To be accursed is to be cut off from God. Of this alienation the darkness that covered the land that first Good Friday afternoon was symbolic (Matt. 27:45).

"My God, my God, why have you forsaken me?" Does not the very address of this cry ring with a strange sound on the lips of Jesus? Jesus always addressed God as "Father." So he prayed in that first word when the soldiers hammered his quivering flesh to the cross: "Father, forgive them; for they do not know what they are doing" (Luke 23:34). So he would pray soon again in his last word: "Father, into your hands I commend my spirit" (Luke 23:46).

But not now in this fourth word. He had not, of course, ceased to be God the Son. He remained one in his being with the Father as the Second Person of the Trinity. But he had been cut off from all fellowship with the Father, from all expressions of his love, from all the rights and privileges of a son that he had enjoyed without so much as a moment's interruption from all eternity. Now he hung between earth and heaven with no home in either. His Father's smile was hidden. His Father's favor was withdrawn. Laden with the sins of others, the sinless One sank into the lowest depths of hell as the waves and billows of God's wrath swept over him.

John Duncan was a divinity professor in Edinburgh, Scotland, more than a century ago. A master of Hebrew, he was

called Rabbi Duncan by his students. Referring to Psalm 22:1
in class one day, he asked his students, "Ay, ay, d'ye know
what it was—dying on the cross, forsaken by His Father—
d'ye know what it was? What! What! . . . It was *damnation*—
and He took it *lovingly*."

No wonder Jesus felt God-abandoned! He *was* God-abandoned! That is why his cry of dereliction shivered to the sky.

The Words
from God's Perspective

A little girl once listened to a sermon on the death of
Christ. As she left the church, she said, "Mommy, I love
Jesus but I hate God." We must be careful not to create false
impressions of God the Father when we talk about the death
of Christ.

On the cross Jesus endured God's wrath against sin. That,
as we have seen, is what this cry of abandonment means.
But—and mark it carefully—we must not suppose that God
was angry with Jesus. Angry with the sin that he bore? Yes!
Angry with the Son who bore it? Never!

How could God be angry with his Son? Twice—first at
Jesus' baptism at the beginning of his ministry, and then at
his transfiguration toward its close—God himself testified,
"This is my Son, the Beloved, with whom I am well pleased"
(Matt. 3:17; 17:5).

Jesus went to the cross in obedience to his Father's will.
Had he not prayed in Gethsemane only a few hours before,
"My Father, if it is possible, let this cup pass from me; yet not
what I want but what you want" (Matt. 26:39)? In his
Pentecost sermon Peter declared that Jesus was delivered up
to death according to the plan and purpose of God (Acts
2:23). His offering up of himself upon the cross was his
crowning act of obedience. Never was any son or daughter so
pleasing to their father as Jesus was to his Father when this
cry of dereliction burst forth from his fevered lips. On the
cross Jesus suffered the effect of God's anger, his judgment

on sin which you and I deserve, but he did not suffer God's displeasure toward himself.

⎧ It is not true to say, as some have done, that God was never closer to Jesus than when he felt himself forsaken. But it certainly is true to say that never did the Father love him more dearly than then. ⎭

Think what this means. What is the one thing above everything else that loving parents never want to do to their child? Is it not this: to hurt that child? To cause that child pain? Is that not what makes child abuse so heinous?

When I was a boy, I managed to get myself punished fairly often. I can still hear my father, yardstick in hand, saying to me, "This hurts me more than it hurts you." Somehow I never found those words very convincing—never, that is, until I became a parent and had to punish my own children. I would rather have punished myself. True love always tries to shield its beloved from pain at any cost.

You remember God's command to Abraham to offer his son Isaac as a sacrifice. I think everyone I've ever heard tell that story stressed most how difficult it was for Abraham to obey God's command as he raised the knife to plunge it into Isaac's heart. But what about Isaac? After all, he was the victim. It was his life, not Abraham's, that God required. Yet in spite of all that, it is a true instinct of love that feels most keenly the pain and anguish of Abraham.

What shall we say then about the Father of our Lord Jesus Christ when he delivered his one and only Son, whom he dearly loved and in whom he delighted from all eternity, to the cruelest death ever devised by the depraved mind of man? What shall we say about him when he abandoned that sinless Son to the deepest depths of hell for sins that were not his?

You may be familiar with the acrostic definition of grace:

G - God's
R - Riches
A - At
C - Christ's
E - Expense.

It is a clever acrostic, but it is bad theology. Could God deliver his own Son to hell and never feel even a flicker of pain? Do you recall David's lament when news reached him of the death of Absalom, the rebellious son who had stolen his throne and driven him into exile? "O my son Absalom! My son, my son Absalom! If only I had died instead of you—O Absalom, my son, my son!" (2 Sam. 18:33 niv). Is it conceivable that God the Father suffered no pain like that when Jesus' cry of dereliction came screaming to his throne in heaven? Of course not! And when we read that "God was in Christ reconciling the world to Himself" (2 Cor. 5:19 nasb), we know that when his wrath broke upon his Son, it broke his own heart, too.

The Words
from the Believer's Perspective

Thanks be to God, these words assure us who are believers that in Christ we have been *redeemed* forever from God's judgment on our sin. "There is therefore now no condemnation for those who are in Christ Jesus," exclaims Paul (Rom. 8:1). Christ endured the full penalty of our sin and satisfied all the claims of God's justice against us. He drained the cup, of God's wrath bone dry, leaving not a drop for us to drink. We are acquitted, pardoned, forgiven—completely and forever. Augustus Toplady, author of the hymn "Rock of Ages," puts it well:

> If Thou hast my discharge procured,
> And freely in my room endured
>   The whole of wrath divine,
> Payment God cannot twice demand,
> First at my bleeding Surety's hand,
>   And then again at mine.

These words also assure us that in Christ we have been *reconciled* to God. He endured our alienation from God, so that he might make peace for us with God. "Christ also suffered for sins once for all," says Peter, "the righteous for the unrighteous, in order to bring you to God" (1 Pet. 3:18). "Behold," cried John the Baptist as Jesus passed by, "the Lamb of God, who takes away the sin of the world!" (John 1:29 RSV). Jesus not only took our sin upon himself; he took it away. He removed it from us and from God's sight forever.

A dazzled world looked on in wonderment when the Berlin Wall, which for twenty-five years stood as an ugly symbol of the hostility between the communistic countries of Eastern Europe and the free world, suddenly came tumbling down on November 9, 1989, its destruction bringing the promise of new friendship between East and West. At Calvary the wall of sin that separated us from the all-holy God was demolished once and for all. In a mystery forever baffling to our minds Christ was abandoned by God that we might be restored to God. The Son of God became an outcast from God that we might become sons and daughters of God, knowing his love, rejoicing in his favor, now and for all eternity:

> The Holy One did hide His face;
>   O Christ, 'twas hid from Thee!
> Dumb darkness wrapt Thy soul a space,
>   The darkness due to me;
> But now that face of radiant grace
>   Shines out in love on me.

And then, we find in this cry of dereliction a powerful *restraint* against sin and a powerful *motivation* to righteousness. "He himself bore our sins"—remember, that means bore their penalty—"in his body on the cross," says Peter, "so that, free from sins, we might live for righteousness" (1 Pet. 2:24).

In *Joseph and His Brethren*, Thomas Mann suggests several influences that steadied Joseph against the charms and wiles of Potiphar's wife. But, says Mann, when the full fury of the crisis broke on him, the decisive influence was the memory of his father Jacob's face. It was the memory of that face, more than anything else, that held him to the royal road of moral purity.

"My God, my God, why have you forsaken me?" There is nothing in Christian experience, except the power of the Holy Spirit, that will so strengthen us to resist the fierce, subtle allurements of sin and spur us on to nobler living as the echo of that cry ringing in our souls.

Redemption, reconciliation, restraint against sin, and motivation to righteousness—for us as Christians all these, and nothing less, lie wrapped up in this cry of the Crucified.

The Words
from the Unbeliever's Perspective

On the one hand, these words strike the most solemn warning God has ever given to those who have not turned from their sins to Christ for salvation.

Whatever Happened to Hell? was published a few years ago. It would be hard, would it not, to choose a title that captures more arrestingly the temper of our times? Multitudes of people today live carefree, frivolous lives, never giving half a second's thought to the solemn concerns of eternity. A glance at their map of the universe explains everything. There is no location on it marked "hell." And they don't worry that NASA's Hubble Space Telescope might send back photos of it, either. Judging from what they do on Sunday mornings, we are surrounded by a whole colony of them in our neighborhood. You may be, too.

As far as these people are concerned, hell, if ever there was such a place, vanished with Adam and Eve and the talking snake, assuming they have heard of them. After all, everybody knows that God—if there is a God—would never send anyone to hell except maybe a few reprobates like Hitler, Stalin, and Al Capone. He is far too tolerant and loving ever to do a thing like that.

I confess that often when I think about the destiny of unbelievers—especially loved ones and friends and those who struggle to live decent, moral lives—I wish I could embrace the rosy creed of universalism. (But is it really rational to believe that if God abandoned his own Son to hell when he offered himself as a sacrifice for the sins of others, that he will refuse to abandon to hell those who persist in their own sins and unbelief? Will he refrain from punishing those who will have nothing to do with his Son? Who spurn his love? Who ignore his claims? Who don't want his salvation? Who trample his blood under their feet?)

(What kind of God would he be if he did that? Could you respect him? Could you call him just? Could you believe that he is really love? That God should pour out his wrath on his sinless Son when he died for sinners, but not on rebellious, impenitent, unbelieving sinners themselves outrages all sense of moral decency and right. When I look at that bloody, battered, broken figure on Golgotha's cross, and when I hear him scream from the depths of hell, "My God, my God, why have you forsaken me?" I realize what a monster God would be if he let everyone into heaven in the end. But he won't.)

(It is said that in his dying hour Voltaire, the French philosopher and author and one of Christianity's worst foes, shrieked, "I am abandoned by God!" When I read this text, I am not surprised.)

But these words also sound an appeal. In them we hear the Savior's most earnest, most tender plea to every sinner to receive from him the forgiveness he purchased at such incalculable cost, to take refuge from the tidal waves of divine wrath and retribution in his cross. For in the whole vast universe—and astronomers tell us it is getting bigger all the time—there is no place of safety, but here.

"My God, my God, why have you forsaken me?" A solemn warning of the unbelieving sinner's doom, and a loving, urgent entreaty to find deliverance from it in the Crucified of God. This is what God wants you if you are outside of Christ to hear in this cry.

God forsaken by God! The Son of God damned by his Father for all who believe in him! The sinless One condemned by his Father to the sinner's hell! Mystery of mysteries, indeed! What it meant for both Father and Son we shall never fully know. But nothing less than this could purchase our pardon and bring us home to God. How, then, can we who have received his salvation fail to give this Savior what he wants the most—the undivided love and loyalty of our hearts?

> Were the whole realm of nature mine,
>   That were an offering far too small;
> Love so amazing, so divine,
>   Demands my life, my soul, my all!

Will you solemnly covenant now by his grace to give him that and nothing less from this day forward, so long as you shall live?

His are the thousand sparkling rills
That from a thousand fountains burst,
And fill with music all the hills:
And yet he saith, "I thirst."

All fiery pangs on battlefields,
On fever beds where sick men toss,
Are in that human cry he yields
To anguish on the Cross.

But more than pains that racked him then
Was the deep longing thirst divine
That thirsted for the souls of men:
Dear Lord! and one was mine.

O Love most patient, give me grace;
Make all my soul athirst for thee:
That parched dry lip, that fading face,
That thirst, were all for me.

—Cecil Frances Alexander

5

The Thirsty Christ

Herschel H. Hobbs

After this, Jesus knowing that all things were now accomplished, that the scripture might be fulfilled, saith, "I thirst." (John 19:28 KJV)

Darkness at noon! Some say it was caused by a dust storm. But it was too dark for that. Others attribute it to an eclipse of the sun. But it was the time of the full moon when that, too, would have been impossible. The darkness at noon was nature rebelling against what sinful men were doing to nature's God. The sun refused to shine.

In the eerie darkness the ribald mob suddenly became silent. What had they done? Perhaps the only sound was an occasional groan from those crucified. Near the end of this three-hour period, the darkness was pierced by Jesus' cry of dereliction as he suffered the agony of the doomed and damned—for us. The atonement was accomplished. And the darkness fled away.

Meanwhile, John had returned from taking Jesus' mother

to his own home. Apparently once again he stood at the foot of Jesus' cross. Doing so, he evidently heard Jesus speak. For he is the only one who reports it.

Jesus spoke one word. *Dipsō*, "I thirst." More than fifty years later, looking back to that moment, John interprets this word. Although his primary purpose in writing his Gospel is to emphasize the union of deity and humanity in Jesus, John also supplements the other three Gospels. Throughout his Gospel he uses the phrases "after this" and "after these things." These phrases seem to be a formula indicating at given points that he is inserting events not recorded in the other Gospels. Matthew 27:46 and Mark 15:34 record the cry of dereliction. They also relate that someone pressed to Jesus' lips a sponge filled with "vinegar" or sour wine. But they do not give the reason for it. John explains why this was done. It was in response to Jesus' words, "I thirst."

John also interprets the reason Jesus uttered these words at this point: "Jesus knowing that all things were now accomplished, that the scripture might be fulfilled, saith, 'I thirst.'" "Fulfilled" and "accomplished" translate kindred Greek words. "Fulfilled" means to reach a goal, to accomplish a task or mission. In this case the reference is to Jesus' redemptive mission. "Accomplished" means to perform the last act in completing a task—like driving the final nail in a house, placing the last brick in a wall, or writing the ending word of a poem. It is exactly the word translated, "It is finished," in verse 30.

Throughout the Gospels notice is taken of Old Testament prophecies fulfilled in Jesus' life and ministry. In the context of the cross interpreters rightly point to Psalm 69:21: "They gave me also gall for my meat; and in my thirst they gave me vinegar to drink."

But to me a far richer field in this regard is Psalm 22. Approximately a thousand years before the event, the Holy Spirit enabled David to describe the crucifixion of Jesus as if he were witnessing it in person. For instance, the cry of dereliction is the opening verse of Psalm 22. Note further: soldiers gambled for Jesus' clothes (22:18); passersby mocked him (22:7); the mob jeered him (22:12–13); they pierced his hands and feet (22:16), so that his life flowed out like water (22:14); his rib bones could be counted as he was stretched out on the cross (22:14, 17); the members of the Sanhedrin quoted Psalm 22:8; and following his death the soldiers found that his heart had ruptured (22:14; John 19:33–34). In citing the prophecies we also must not overlook Isaiah 53:4–6.

So John notes that all these prophecies had been fulfilled. But one remained: "My strength is dried up like a potsherd; and my tongue cleaveth to my jaws; and thou hast brought me into the dust of death" (Ps. 22:15). Therefore, in performing the last act fulfilling the prophecies concerning his death, Jesus says, "I thirst."

Now let it be noted that in his death Jesus was not merely waltzing through make-believe that he might check off the prophecies. To the contrary, the Old Testament writers wrote more than they knew. The Holy Spirit enabled them to portray in advance the grim reality of the price Jesus paid for the sins of the world.

With these analytical matters behind us, three questions call for answers: Why did Jesus utter this word? Why did John record it? What does it say to us?

Why Jesus Uttered This Word

First, Jesus said, "I thirst," for the obvious reason that he was thirsty. Dehydration was one of the most terrible sufferings associated with crucifixion. It is possible, insofar as we can tell from the Gospel records, that eighteen hours had passed since Jesus had had something to drink. Even before he was nailed to the cross, the ordeal through which he had gone had taken its toll. According to Luke, the physician, in Gethsemane his sweat was like great drops of blood. Scourging by the soldiers had left his back a bloody mass. The crown of thorns had pierced his brow, causing further loss of blood.

Jesus was crucified naked. The six-hour ordeal on the cross had dehydrated his body. Every sunbeam became a leech sucking more life-sustaining moisture from his body. Every pore of his skin became a flowing fountain.

Loss of liquid produced great fever. In fact, the word for "thirst" is found in the papyri in medical reports in connection with fever. Because of such high fever Jesus' lips were parched. His eyeballs burned in their sockets. His head ached with excruciating pain. His mouth became as dry as cotton. His tongue became swollen. Inflamed vocal cords made his voice husky, almost like a croak.

With the atonement finished, Jesus showed the first evidence of concern for his own physical condition. Even then it was not really for his own sake. He was ready to utter his cry of victory. He did not want it to be an inaudible croak. It must sound like a trumpet. Therefore, his inflamed vocal cords must for just a moment be cooled. His tongue must be able to verbalize that victory shout. So Jesus said, "I thirst."

I do not doubt for a moment that Jesus could have come down from the cross to find water to drink. He *could*, but he *would* not do so. Instead, he would endure the cross to the end.

A compassionate soldier fastened a sponge to a hyssop reed, dipped it in a sour wine drunk by soldiers on duty, and with it moistened Jesus' mouth. I have often wondered: Had I been there, would I have performed this deed of mercy? Would you? Little did the soldier know that he fulfilled prophecy that day. Notice how the suffering Savior had already begun to soften hardened hearts. The soldier gave Jesus only a few drops of cooling liquid. But they were enough.

Still from the cross Jesus asks, "Is it nothing to you, all ye that pass by? behold, and see if there be any sorrow like unto my sorrow, which is done unto me" (Lam. 1:12). Let us look on him whom we have pierced (Zech. 12:10; John 19:37) and believe.

Why John Recorded This Word

John recorded this word because it happened. But as so often, when we look beneath the surface of Jesus' words, we see a deeper meaning. These words declare the humanity of Jesus.

To understand this we must examine the thought patterns of an ancient philosophy called Gnosticism. It was a combination of Greek philosophy, Hebrew theology, and Oriental mysticism.

The Gnostics held that God is absolutely good and matter is absolutely evil. Their problem was how to explain the origin of the universe. They taught that an absolutely good God could not create an absolutely evil universe. So they imagined a series of beings emanating from God in descending order, each being with less deity than the one above it. The lowest being had enough deity to create, but so little as to be able to create evil matter. When the Gnostics came into contact with Christianity, they identified Christ as this lowest being.

Furthermore, the Gnostics were divided in their views of the nature of Jesus Christ. The docetic Gnostics ("docetic" comes from the Greek word *dokeō*, meaning, "I seem") said that Christ did not have a flesh and blood body. He only *seemed* to have one. The Cerinthian Gnostics (named for their leader Cerinthus) said that Christ was not born, neither did he die. The person of Christ came upon Jesus at his baptism and left him on the cross. The docetic Gnostics denied the humanity of Christ; the Cerinthian Gnostics denied the deity of Jesus. To deny one is as great a heresy as to deny the other. This philosophy cut right through Christian belief about Jesus Christ.

The words, "I thirst," show that Jesus Christ did have a flesh and blood body. John already declares this truth at the beginning of his Gospel: "And the Word [Christ] was made [became] flesh" (John 1:14). "Became" means that he became something which he never before had been—a flesh and blood man. John 1:17 says, "For the law was given by [*dia*, "through"] Moses, but grace and truth came [*egeneto*, "became"] by [*dia*, "through"] Jesus Christ." In other words, when God gave his law, he did so through a man—Moses. When he revealed his grace and truth he became a man—Jesus of Nazareth. This is not to deny Jesus' deity. Rather it stresses deity in humanity. As Jesus was fully God, so also he was fully man. He was and still is the God-man.

Jesus' favorite self-designation was "Son of man." Although this was a messianic title, to the Jewish mind, it would carry no military-political overtones as did the title "Messiah" or "Christ." Furthermore, it stressed Jesus' relation to humanity.

In his humanity Jesus completely identified with us, apart from sin. He grew tired, hungry, and thirsty. He needed sleep. He could be in only one place at a time. If he went from Galilee to Jerusalem, he had to walk every step of the way. Although wiser than any other person, he voluntarily accepted a certain limitation of knowledge. When he is said to have marveled at people's unbelief, "marveled" means to wonder without understanding. As a man he said that even he did not know the time of his second coming (Mark 13:32).

In his humanity Jesus could be tempted (Matt. 4:1–11; Luke 4:1–13). Speaking of his incarnation, the author of Hebrews says, "For verily he took not on him the nature of angels; but he took on him the seed of Abraham. Wherefore in all things it behoved him to be made like unto his brethren, that he might be a merciful and faithful high priest in things pertaining to God, to make reconciliation for the sins of the people. For in that he himself hath suffered being tempted, he is able to succour them that are tempted" (Heb. 2:16–18).

The same writer also says, "For we have not an high priest which cannot be touched with the feeling of our infirmities; but was in all points tempted like as we are, yet without sin. Let us therefore come boldly unto the throne of grace, that we may obtain mercy, and find grace to help in time of need" or "in the nick of time" (Heb. 4:15–16).

Yes, Jesus was tempted in every respect as we are—"yet

without sin." In Luke 4:13 we read, "And when the devil had ended all the temptation, he departed from him for a season." In the Greek text, "every" is without the definite article. So it means "every kind of temptation."

You have not known any temptation that Jesus did not know. This means that he could have yielded to them. Thinking only of Jesus' deity, some people draw back in horror from this thought. But remember that he was also human. If he could not yield to temptation, then he merely pretended to be tempted. This means that he was a hypocrite, a sin which he himself condemned unmercifully (see Matt. 23).

It is true that "God cannot be tempted with evil" (James 1:13). But remember that Jesus was and is the God-man. This mystery defies human understanding, to be sure. But it is a fact of Scripture.

Yes, in his humanity Jesus had the potential of yielding. But, praise God, he also had the power not to yield! He was tempted in all points as we are, *yet without sin.* There is not a single mistake of Jesus in the trophy hall of Satan!

Who knows better the power of temptation? The one who yields after the first skirmish? Or the one who endures and fights through to victory? Obviously, the latter. Jesus did that. So he knows what it means for you when you are tempted. And he can enable you to resist every kind of temptation—if only you will yield to him and come without fear to the throne of grace to find help in the time of need.

Each one of Jesus' wilderness temptations was designed to lead him to avoid the cross. The temptation to do that came to him again and again (Matt. 16:21–23; John 6:14–15). It came for the final time through members of the Sanhedrin. They challenged Jesus to "come down from the cross, and we will believe (you)" (Matt. 27:41–42).

But still Jesus did not yield. He remained on the cross until the atonement was complete (Matt. 27:46). Then, and only then, he said, "I thirst."

Paul expresses it thus: "that (God) might be just, and the justifier of him which believeth in Jesus" (Rom. 3:26b). All have sinned and come short of God's glory (Rom. 3:23). By

his life Jesus proved that God is just in his demands for righteousness on our part. Having done so, as the God-man he
endured the cross to enable God to be the justifier of all who
believe in Jesus. For "God was in Christ, reconciling the
world unto himself" (2 Cor. 5:19a).

What This Word Says to Us

The Greek verb *dipsō* is in the present tense, expressing
continuous action. "I keep on thirsting." On the cross Jesus
was physically thirsty. He was also spiritually thirsty, thirsty
for the souls of lost people. And he keeps on thirsting for lost
souls today. That is why he died on the cross in the first
place. And he will keep on thirsting so long as there is one
soul who does not believe in him as Savior.

At the cross a soldier sought to quench Jesus' physical
thirst. We must continue to quench his spiritual thirst. If you
have never believed in him as your personal Savior, you can
help quench it by receiving him as your Savior now.
Christians can help quench this thirst by leading other souls
to receive him as Savior and Lord. On the cross he did all
that he could do to save the lost. And he has committed to
us the responsibility of sharing the gospel with lost people
everywhere. He is able and willing to save. But he waits on
his people, on you and me, to carry the good news to the
world.

> The soul of Jesus is restless (thirsty) today;
> Christ is tramping through the spirit-world,
> Compassion in His heart for the fainting millions;
> He trudges through China, through Poland,
> Through Russia, Austria, Germany, Armenia;
> Patiently He pleads with the Church,
> Tenderly He woos her.
> The wounds of His body are bleeding afresh for the
>   sorrows of His shepherdless people.
> We besiege Him with selfish petitions,
> We weary Him with our petty ambitions,

From the needy we bury Him in piles of carven stone,
We obscure Him in the smoke of stuffy incense,
We drown His voice with the snarls and shrieks of our
    disgruntled bickerings,
We build temples to Him with hands that are bloody,
We deny Him in the needs and sorrows of the exploited—
    "least of His brethren."
The soul of Jesus is restless (thirsty) today,
But eternally undismayed.

My Soul Thirsts for God

I thirst, but not as I once did,
The vain delights of earth to share;
Thy wounds, Emmanuel, all forbid
That I should seek my pleasures there.

It was the sight of Thy dear cross
First weaned my soul from earthly things
And taught me to esteem as dross
The mirth of fools, and pomp of kings.

I want that grace that springs from Thee,
That quickens all things where it flows,
And makes a wretched thorn like me
Bloom as myrtle or the rose.

Dear fountain of delights unknown!
No longer sink below the brim,
But overflow and pour me down
A living and life-giving stream!

For sure, of all the plants that share
The notice of Thy Father's eye,
None proves less grateful to His care
Or yields him meaner fruit than I.

—William Cowper

Hark! the voice of love and mercy
Sounds aloud from Calvary;
See, it rends the rocks asunder,
Shakes the earth, and veils the sky:
"It is finished!" "It is finished!" "It is finished!"
Hear the dying Saviour cry;
Hear the dying Saviour cry.

"It is finished!" O what pleasure
Do these precious words afford;
Heav'nly blessings, without measure,
Flow to us from Christ the Lord:
"It is finished!" "It is finished!" "It is finished!"
Saints the dying words record;
Saints the dying words record.

Finished all the types and shadows
Of the ceremonial law;
Finished all that God had promised;
Death and hell no more shall awe:
"It is finished!" "It is finished!" "It is finished!"
Saints, from hence your comfort draw;
Saints, from hence your comfort draw.

Tune your harps anew, ye seraphs,
Join to sing the glorious theme;
All in earth, and all in heaven,
Join to praise Emmanuel's Name:
Alleluia! Alleluia! Alleluia!
Glory to the bleeding Lamb!
Glory to the bleeding Lamb!

—Jonathan Evans

6

It Is Finished!

George C. Fuller

"It is finished." (John 19:30 NIV)

Jesus may have died on Friday, April 6, A.D. 30. His execution attracted some devoted followers, now confused and uncertain. Golgotha is not pleasant, no more so than the place of the gallows, or guillotine, or electric chair, or gas chamber. But morbid curiosity assures attendance.

Jesus' enemies were there, those who yearned for his death, to get him out of their way. The civil authorities, soldiers and others, carried out their orders. Curious but indifferent crowds passed by. Although crucifixions were never quite the same, this one seemed different, strange. At noon the sun stopped shining and darkness was everywhere. Piercing the shadows and silence, a shout came from the man on the middle cross: "It is finished!" A few minutes later he died.

What Jesus' Words Meant to God

Jesus had always claimed a unique relationship with God. God was the Father of all Israel and is the Father of all believers. His people are "children of God." But Jesus spoke of God as *his own* Father. John 5 begins the record of claims that led to his death: "As the Father has life in himself, so he has granted the Son to have life in himself. . . . And the Father who sent me has himself testified concerning me. . . . These are the Scriptures that testify about me; yet you refuse to come to me to have life" (John 5:26, 37, 39b–40). These kinds of claims to a special relationship with the Father were met with a plot to kill Jesus. Now, on the cross, Jesus shouts in death, "It is finished!" How did the Father understand these words?

In the first place, he hears Jesus say, "Your word is fulfilled!" The word here is the Bible, particularly, of course, the Hebrew Scriptures, our Old Testament. "All of the predictions, all of the foreshadowing, all of the prayers and hopes and dreams of your people are brought to completion here on the cross, now."

Understandably, a reader may ask, "Why is the issue of the Bible and prophecy brought into this discussion, and so early?" Perhaps it betrays the interests of the writer and his own agenda. But recall Jesus' reprimand of the disciple who sought to prevent his arrest: "Put your sword back in its place. . . . Do you think I cannot call on my Father, and he will at once put at my disposal more than twelve legions of angels? But how then would the Scriptures be fulfilled that say it must happen in this way?" (Matt. 26:52–54). Jesus rejected any effort in his defense, because he must go to death on the cross, all in accord with the plan of Scripture.

In the first two chapters of Matthew's Gospel, we are reminded that events in the life of Jesus fulfilled biblical prophecy. A number of specific Old Testament references are cited: "'the virgin will be with child and will give birth to a son, and they will call him Immanuel.' . . . 'Out of Egypt I called my son.' . . . 'A voice is heard in Ramah, weeping and great mourning, Rachel weeping for her children and refusing to be comforted, because they are no more.' . . . 'He will be called a Nazarene'" (Matt. 1:23; 2:15, 18, 23b).

Jesus' entire life was a fulfillment, even to the end. Just before our text at the end of the Gospels, the note of fulfilled prophecy is rung out again. The soldiers are arguing over Jesus' robe. Look at verse 24: "'Let's not tear it', they said to one another. 'Let's decide by lot who will get it.'" Then John adds, "This happened that the scripture might be fulfilled which said, 'They divided my garments among them and cast lots for my clothing.'" The quotation is from Psalm 22:18.

Perhaps the last act of fulfillment in Jesus' life is found immediately before his shout, "It is finished!" Look at verse 28: "Later, knowing that all was now completed, and so that the Scripture would be fulfilled, Jesus said, 'I am thirsty.'" What follows acts out the script of what is perhaps the last Old Testament prophecy fulfilled in the life of Jesus. "They put gall in my food and gave me vinegar for my thirst" (Ps. 69:21). The same Greek word, translated "fulfilled," "completed," "finished," is used three times in the verses now before us. Jesus' word (v. 30), "It is finished," is found twice in verse 28 ("all things are finished"; "the Scripture is finished").

Of course, his death is not the end of the story; there is resurrection, rule, return. But all of the Word of God concerning his birth, life, and sacrificial death is fulfilled, completed, by three o'clock that Friday afternoon. Later, he will make this clear to his disciples: "This is what I told you while I was still with you: Everything must be fulfilled that is written about me in the Law of Moses, the Prophets and the Psalms. . . . This is what is written: The Christ will suffer and rise from the dead on the third day, and repentance and forgiveness of sins will be preached in his name to all nations, beginning at Jerusalem" (Luke 24:44, 46–47).

"It is finished!" the Savior shouts. And the Father hears, "Your word is fulfilled!" But he also hears this: "Your will is accomplished!"

In the plan of God the cross was necessary. It always was from the beginning. The sin of Adam, the sin of people, your sin, my sin did not come as a surprise to God, so that he had to change plans that he had already put into place. From all eternity God the Father and God the Son had planned, had made a covenant between themselves. The goal of their plan was to apply grace and mercy to sin. Listen to a portion of Paul's discussion of God's plan in Ephesians 1: "He (God the Father) chose us in him (Jesus) before the creation of the world to be holy and blameless in his sight. . . . In him (Jesus) we have redemption through his blood, the forgiveness of sins, in accordance with the riches of God's grace" (Eph. 1:4, 7). God the Father understands God the Son to be shouting from that cross, "Your will is accomplished!"

Throughout his life, Jesus made it clear that he had been sent from another place, that he had come from Someone, to accomplish a purpose, a goal, a work that had been assigned to him. He said, "the Son of Man did not come to be served, but to serve, and to give his life as a ransom for many" (Mark 10:45); "the Son of Man came to seek and to save what was lost" (Luke 19:10). Jesus understood that he had been sent for a purpose and with a mission: to accomplish the work of redeeming his people.

In his commitment to that cause, Jesus knew that he was identifying his deeds, his work, his life, and his death with his Father's will for him. At one point Jesus made this clear to his disciples: "My food is to do the will of him who sent me and to finish his work" (John 4:34). In the fifth chapter of John's Gospel, Jesus clearly identifies his mission with that of the Father, and claims a unique personal relationship with the Father. He does this so clearly that the Pharisees intensify their plans to kill him, not only for breaking the Sabbath but for making himself equal with the Father. His testimony is summarized in John 5:30: "I seek not to please myself but him who sent me." Hear that theme repeated: "For I have come down from heaven, not to do my will but to do the will of him who sent me" (John 6:38). Hear his prayer of agony in the garden: "Father, if you are willing, take this cup from me; yet not my will, but yours be done" (Luke 22:42).

The humble birth, the life of rejection, the ultimate death were all pieces of the plan, the will of the Father for the Son. And Jesus the Son willfully, willingly, obediently submitted. He who was "in very nature God, did not consider equality with God something to be grasped, but made himself nothing, taking the very nature of a servant, being made in human likeness. And being found in appearance as a man, he humbled himself and became obedient to death—even death on a cross" (Phil. 2:6–8). He voluntarily submitted to the will of the Father, even though he was one with the Father. As the author of Hebrews says, "although he was a son, he learned obedience from what he suffered" (Heb. 5:8).

Who crucified Jesus? Whose will was fulfilled on the cross? If that is a multiple-choice question, all of these answers would be correct: Satan (he was behind the plotting of the Pharisees), the Pharisees, Pilate, the soldiers, the people.

Nor, of course, can we forget Judas. He, too, was responsible for the cross. Jesus said about Judas, "The Son of Man will go as it has been decreed, but woe to that man who betrays him" (Luke 22:22). Ultimately, however, the will of the Father alone was the cause for the cross of Jesus. When Peter sought to prevent Jesus' arrest, Jesus declared, "Put your sword away! Shall I not drink the cup the Father has given me?" (John 18:11). Yet it was not the will of Satan, or Pilate, or Judas that required the cross. It was the will of the Father, finally and ultimately, that Jesus obeyed from birth to death, even to his death on the cross.

Other men die. Jesus came to die! This is why he was born. The name he was given (in Hebrew "Joshua," meaning perhaps "the Lord, our deliverer") spoke of his mission. The angel told the shepherds, "Today in the town of David a Savior has been born to you" (Luke 2:11a). He could not, he did not want to, escape the significance of that name and the demand of that mission: to give himself for his people. Jesus said: "The Son of man came to seek and to save what was lost" (Luke 19:10). Paul could look back and summarize the entire drama: "Christ Jesus came into the world to save sinners" (1 Tim. 1:15b).

The Father is portrayed as far more than a passive, distant, disinterested observer. His voice of approval and anointing breaks through at the baptism of Jesus: "This is my Son, whom I love; with him I am well pleased" (Matt. 3:17). Out of the cloud, on the mount of transfiguration, the same message comes from heaven: "This is my Son, whom I love; with him I am well pleased. Listen to him!" (Matt. 17:5b). A major theme of the New Testament is that the cross of Jesus is a completed work. The will of God is fulfilled there for the deliverance of his people from sin. Of course, this event must be seen in light of the resurrection. It is not defeat, but victory. It represents the completion of all that is necessary for the salvation of God's people.

What Jesus' Words Mean for Us

First of all, these words mean, "Jesus is victorious!" It certainly did not appear that way. "Victory" was hardly a word that anyone would associate with capital punishment, death at the hands of the religious and civil authorities. Other things come to mind—defeat, disaster, loss, sorrow—but certainly not victory.

After the resurrection Jesus talked with two men as they walked together on the road from Jerusalem to Emmaus. The Bible indicates that they were kept from recognizing Jesus (Luke 24:16). Perhaps their sad comments about what had happened reflected the crushed hopes of Jesus' disciples: he was "a prophet, powerful in word and deed before God and all the people. The chief priests and our rulers handed him over to be sentenced to death, and they crucified him; but we had hoped that he was the one who was going to redeem Israel" (Luke 24:19–21). Some historians have seen Jesus as a disillusioned prophet, some kind of misguided messiah whose death was tragic defeat. That is certainly the way it appeared.

Anyone who had some understanding of the warfare that had been waged between Jesus and Satan might reasonably have thought, "It's all over; Satan wins!" His disciples might have thought back to what they knew of Jesus' temptation, when the wicked power of Satan was overcome by the determined will of the Messiah. Or they might have recalled their own experience in confronting the rule of Satan and his forces, as, for example, when they returned to Jesus in triumph, saying, "Lord, even the demons submit to us in your name" (Luke 10:17b). They surely remembered the continuing conflict with the religious leaders over Jesus' power and authority. Was it from Satan or from God? Now, Friday afternoon, April 6, A.D. 30, appears to be Satan's finest hour. The Son of Man, the Son of God is on the cross dying, dead. That is the way it appears: Jesus loses, Satan wins. But that's not the way it is.

"It is finished!" is not a scream of agony, the anguished cry of final defeat. Matthew, Mark, and Luke speak of a "great shout," perhaps referring to these words. It is the conqueror's cry of victory. The pain is completed, the plan fulfilled. There is no more betrayal of Judas, no more denial by Peter, no more attacks from the priests, no more mocking before Pilate. No more humiliation, no more conflict, no more suffering. The time of suffering and sorrow is at an end. The Father's cup has been emptied, his will fulfilled. It is the moment of great victory, not because death is the end, but because death is why he came. He exchanges the shabby robes of a criminal-king for the royal garments of the Lord of lords and the King of kings.

And what of Satan? He understands, perhaps too late. He hears the words, "It is finished!" and they say to him, "Satan, you lose!" In his temptation of Jesus, Satan offered him food and the kingdoms of this world, and dared Jesus to presume upon the protection of his Father. But "when the devil had finished all this tempting, he left him until an opportune time" (Luke 4:13). Of course, throughout his ministry Jesus continued to struggle with Satan, who worked through demons and through the lives of those who represented him, always seeking to divert Jesus from the will of the Father. "Jesus, help us against Rome," they might say. Or "Jesus, do miracles, so that many others will join with us." Or "Jesus, we will protect you from your enemies; you do not have to die on the cross."

As early in the Gospel record as Mark's first chapter, we see the clash of kingdom against kingdom, King against king, as Jesus casts a demon out of a man in the synagogue. The man cries out, "'What do you want with us, Jesus of Nazareth? Have you come to destroy us? I know who you are—the Holy One of God.' 'Be quiet!' said Jesus sternly. 'Come out of him!' The evil spirit shook the man violently and came out of him with a shriek. The people were all so amazed that they asked each other, 'What is this? A new teaching—and with authority! He even gives orders to evil spirits and they obey him'" (Mark 1:24–27).

Satan wants for himself the people Jesus is saving on the cross. Was it with unrestrained frenzy that Satan continued his attacks against Jesus? "Call legions of angels to defend you. Go into hiding. Let Peter and your friends defend you; let them protect you. Speak up, don't endure the demeaning taunts of Herod. If you really are the Son of God, come down from the cross. If you are who you say you are, save yourself and us." Satan used every scheme of cunning and deceit and blasted away with every cannon at his disposal. Jesus withstood it all. He did what he and the Father had planned to do. He purchased a people for his own possession. He fulfilled the Father's will, and Satan heard the words, "Satan, you lose; Jesus wins."

Jesus' victory and Satan's defeat are complete and assured. But the final application of Jesus' triumph awaits his return in ultimate triumph.

While Satan hears, "You lose," he also hears, "Your days are numbered!" Jesus gave his life as a ransom for many people. During these present days he gathers those people to himself. At the time of the Father's choosing, the process of gathering will end and the Son will return. But during this period, a period of limited duration, Satan, whose defeat is already accomplished and assured, "prowls around like a roaring lion looking for someone to devour" (1 Pet. 5:8b). He wants to wreak havoc in the world. He wants to rule in the hearts of men and women. He wants to bring destruction to life and to lives. But he knows that he is the loser, his time is limited, and his own destruction will come. For the present, however, we must heed the words of Peter: "Resist him, standing firm in the faith, because you know that your brothers throughout the world are undergoing the same kind of sufferings" (1 Pet. 5:9).

The cross, then, was not what it seemed. It appeared to be a tragic defeat for Jesus and the dreams of his disciples. But that apparent tragedy is the culminating act of the obedient and victorious Jesus. The Father's will is fulfilled. Satan loses; Jesus wins. So do his people. Just as Jesus is victorious, his people are also victorious.

It may not have appeared to be a day of victory for Jesus' friends, for the disciples, for Mary. If their grief would have allowed any freedom for thought, they might have said to one another, "We had hoped that he was the one who was going to redeem Israel. But we were wrong. How could they do this to him? How can this be happening?" But appearances are sometimes misleading, never more so than on that afternoon. What appeared to them to be sad defeat was reason for eternal joy and praise.

Jesus was fulfilling the will and plan of the Father on the cross. The covenant of redemption was being completed by the full and sufficient sacrifice of God the Son. The work of redemption is completed, and he shouts out, for the ears of any who will hear, "It is finished!" By that same sacrifice the covenant of grace also is established between the Father and all of the people for whom Jesus died. The benefits of this covenant for God's people are great. They are also secure, safe, and permanent.

We must understand why we need this victory. Sin is the problem. We cannot overestimate the effects of sin in bringing ruin to all of life in God's world and in causing fixed separation between man and God. It is difficult to read the early chapters of Romans and recognize that we are being described there. Only with great difficulty can we picture the human will as deformed and corrupt. How difficult it is to understand that apart from Christ we cannot please God, to know that in us there dwells no good thing.

But to know what our nature really is and to know what Jesus did for us on the cross makes clear why the shout of Jesus, "It is finished!" means victory for us who are believers. All of our sin is forgiven. Our souls which were bleeding like an open wound are healed. Where there was alienation between us and God, there is now reconciliation. All the agonies of life that separate us from him are removed. Satan, with his powerful triumvirate of sin, the law, and death, is defeated. Our immense debt is paid, and we are redeemed from sin. Reconciliation is accomplished. God has justified all of us who have faith in Jesus.

The way into the presence of God is now open. Jesus stands as the head of many who have access to the presence of the Father through him. Perhaps the thief on the cross was the first to hear that news: "I tell you the truth, today you will be with me in paradise" (Luke 23:43). Minutes later the veil of the temple was torn in two (Luke 23:45), indicating that the way was now open for all true worshipers to come before the presence of the Father. Access was available, because the sacrifice of Jesus was finished, complete, perfect. No other sacrifice would suffice, and none is needed. "It is finished!" His work is completed and never needs to be repeated. Contrasting the sacrifice of Jesus with the sacrifices of the Jewish priests, the author of Hebrews writes, "Day after day every priest stands and performs his religious duties; again and again he offers the same sacrifices, which can never take away sins. But when this priest (Jesus) had offered for all time one sacrifice for sins, he sat down at the right hand of God" (Heb. 10:11–12).

Death is no longer the victor. Because of the cross and the resurrection the Christian knows that the words of Isaiah, "He will swallow up death forever" (Isa. 25:8), have been accomplished. So the Christian sings, "Where, O death, is your victory? Where, O death, is your sting? The sting of death is sin, and the power of sin is the law. But thanks be to God! He gives us the victory through our Lord Jesus Christ" (1 Cor. 15:55–57). Death for him was not shame and defeat, but victory. So it is for the believer. Death is not loss, but gain. Because Jesus died, the Christian is victorious.

Like rumbling thunder, the words, "It is finished," roll toward heaven, and the Father hears, "Your word is fulfilled. Your will is accomplished." Through the ages, the people of God, those who belong to Jesus, hear, "Jesus is victorious. We are victorious, too. He wins, and we win!"

But they also ask, "If Jesus has completed that work for me, what works ought I to do for him?" No work needs to be added to the completed work of Calvary: "There is now no condemnation for those who are in Christ Jesus" (Rom. 8:1). Christians rejoice in that assured confidence. But they want to serve the Savior. They ask, "If Jesus has finished the great work of salvation for me, what kind of person should I be? How can I serve him?"

Jesus once explained what it might be like to follow him. He said, "Foxes have holes and birds of the air have nests, but the Son of man has no place to lay his head" (Matt. 8:20). Exactly those last words are used in our text. After he said, "It is finished!" he "lay his head" on his shoulder on the cross in death, and gave up his spirit into the hands of the Father (John 19:30). The time of humiliation is over; his work is done. He rests in death that is like sleep, but is so much more. It is the rest which results from the great work completed, so that he enters the presence of God the Father in triumph.

Until we rest in death, we must be doing the work of him who loved us and gave himself for us. By no means can we expect the path to be easy. It certainly was not easy for Jesus. But we know that the plan of God for our salvation has been completed. We know that, no matter what happens, Jesus is victorious, and in him we are victorious, too. Suppose you are playing in a tough game, perhaps losing badly, and your body aches. How much difference it would make to you in that game, if you knew that eventually your team would win, that the victory was secure, absolutely certain. May Jesus give us grace to live as his people for whom victory is already achieved.

And now, beloved Lord, thy soul resigning
Into thy Father's arms with conscious will,
Calmly, with reverend grace, thy head inclining,
The throbbing brow and labouring breast grow still.

O Lord! o'er mortal agony victorious,
Now is thy triumph! now that Cross shall shine
To earth's remotest age revered and glorious,
Of suffering's deepest mystery the sign.

My Saviour, in mine hour of mortal anguish,
When earth grows dim, and round me falls the night,
O breathe thy peace, as flesh and spirit languish;
At that dread eventide let there be light.

To thy dear Cross turn thou mine eyes in dying;
Lay but my fainting head upon thy breast;
Those outstretched arms receive my latest sighing;
And then, O! then, thine everlasting rest.

—E. S. Alderson

7

The Word of the Winner

Paul S. Rees

Jesus called out with a loud voice, "Father, into your hands I commit my spirit." When he had said this, he breathed his last. (Luke 23:46 NIV)

Behind him now, this God-man, the shouts of angry mobs and the thrust of piercing sword, the close-up curses of his crucifiers and the muffled sobs of his friends and followers.

As the momentary sense of estrangement from God subsides in a hushed realization that God's intention has been fulfilled and God's heaven is opening its doors to him, his voice again grows strong. "Father," he calls, "into your hands I commit my spirit."

The "loud voice" has the resonance not of screaming despair but of unshatterable confidence.

One of Scotland's famous preachers, James Stewart, tells about a little girl who, having lost her mother, would say, every night, "Good night, Father, I'll see you again in the morning." A sad day came when she herself became very ill.

The doctors said she would not recover. Growing weaker by the day, she nevertheless continued her "good nights." Just before she died, her voice now but a whisper, she said it once more: "Good night, Father, I'll see you in the morning!"

Think, now, how easy it would be for the words of our text to fall from Jesus' parched lips. His mind was saturated with the Hebrew Scriptures. Who knows how many times he had quoted Psalm 31:5, "Into your hands I commit my spirit"? To these he had only to add the word of address: "Father."

Surely the crux of this final communication from the dying Jesus is in this verb "commit."

"Commit," at this point, has softer and yet stronger overtones than "submit." The submission speech, contorted with anguish, had been made earlier, in the garden of Gethsemane: "Father, if you are willing, take this cup from me; yet not my will, but yours be done" (Luke 22:42). The pitch of "I submit" is in the direction of resignation. The pitch of "I commit" is in the direction of exultation: "Father, it's all over now. I'm coming home!"

Let's focus on this word "commit" as we find it on the lips of our crucified Lord.

Commencement

Observe, to begin with, that commitment normally has a commencement.

Take the case of Jesus. There was a time when, before human history began, an agreement was reached within the rich pluralism of the Trinity by which the sending Father commissioned the willing Son to visit our errant earth and make a saving atonement for its pride and rebellion.

Admittedly, the biblical details are scarce, but the suggestions given us and the images furnished us have a certain clarity and beauty about them. For example, in Revelation 13:8, Jesus is described as "the Lamb that was slain from the creation of the world." What flashes on the screen of the imagination is heady stuff indeed: the Father in the role of an authority figure and the Son in the role of his obedient agent!

Here is commitment—original, perfect, and purposeful. It is the commitment to act out the role of a sacrificial Lamb offered on the grim altar of the world's guilt—guilt for messing up God's plan for healthy human community and development.

But from the perspective of the Bible we see that before the catastrophe occurred the remedy had been written in the books. Jesus was under contract to visit this planet, as C. S. Lewis liked to put it, and mend the broken pieces.

Let's pause right here and ask ourselves a question: Has our commitment to Christ been recorded in the chronicle of our own experience and in Christ's own "facts-index" as well? If not, when will it be? If not, why not now?

Where life's highest values are concerned, we are now a curiously (even tragically) uncommitted society. Our marriages are reduced to scraps of paper as we walk away from each other at the first disillusionment, or the first burst of anger, or the first personality clash.

Noncommitment is the shameless banner that floats high over the millions of Americans living together without the "inconvenience" of marriage.

Noncommitment is the option chosen by hordes of Americans who belong to the laid-back fraternity of yuppies. Their religion is "meism" and their golden goal is a million or more. No commitment to the poor, the imprisoned, the drug-shackled, the shockingly inferior state of education, the passing on of the good news of Jesus Christ.

Here and there, God be praised, the Christian miracle of shattered selves pulled together around a clean-cut commitment to Christ can be seen—and needs to be seen a thousand times more often.

Here for all the world to see is a Chuck Colson so passionately committed to Jesus that he winces every time some journalist does a verbal snapshot of him as a man who quit politics and now is "into religion," or as a man who "accepted Christianity" while serving time in prison. They cannot see that Colson's commitment is only secondarily to the plight of prisoners and the cause of prison reform, and first, last, and always to Jesus Christ. And forget not, I beg you, that repentance and confession of sin, and a life-and-death trust in the Christ who forgives sin, were the ingredients of Colson's notable commitment.

With few exceptions (the famous Bible teacher G. Campbell Morgan was one) the people who meet Jesus and commit themselves to him, and to the new life he offers, know to the day when the converting transaction took place.

I, for one, know! And I, for one, ask you if you know.

Charles Kingsley, when undecided about choosing whether to live for himself or for God, was down on the south coast of England. One night he went walking alone along the shore. When he returned to his room, he sat down and wrote: "My birthnight! Beside the sleepless sea and beneath the sleeping stars I have given myself to God, a vow, if He gives me the strength I pray for, never to be recalled."

Great business that! It's the essence of commitment in the high moment of commencement.

Continuance

Returning to the text we are examining, consider how commitment, once commenced, calls for continuance.

Clearly, it was so with Jesus.

I stood one day, years ago, at the counter of the city clerk in Minneapolis. A young man next to me was getting a marriage license. When the clerk handed it to him, he asked, "How much does this cost?" With an Irish twinkle in his eyes, the clerk replied, "Two dollars now and as much as you can make for the rest of your life!"

Forgetting the laugh that leaped from the words, I realized that they implied something of far-reaching seriousness. They were saying, "My dear young friend, the vow of commitment that you make in front of the pastor is what you will live with through the long tomorrows, and if it isn't, it might have been better for you if you had stayed away from this

office and kept your $2.00." A timely tune, never more rele-
vant than today.

Think now of the magnificently stretched-out commitment that Jesus made to the Father when he came to live
among us, when he came, as Henry van Dyke puts it, to live
"the human life of God" among us wondering, wooly, ill-
dedicated mortals. Hebrews 10:5, 7 puts it like this: "Therefore, when Christ came into the world, he said: 'Here I am—
it is written about me in the scroll—I have come to do your
will, O God.'"

If we take this as an affirmation of commitment at the
beginning of our Lord's earthly life, then think of his words
near the end. Within hours of his arrest and his being handed
over to his executioners, he prayed to the Father: "I have
brought you glory on earth by completing the work you
gave me to do. . . . I have revealed you to those whom you
gave me. . . . I gave them the words you gave me. . . . I have
given them your word and the world has hated them" (John
17:4, 6, 8, 14).

This is not the wishful thinking of a beginner. It is the
calm, confident testimony of a finisher. It was once commitment accepted; it is now, at priceless cost, commitment
achieved.

What, now, shall we say of our own commitment—to
Christ and his mastery, to a Christ-like life and its daily reality, to the world which he came to rescue and redirect?

Across the English channel from Paris at the time of the
French Revolution lived a starry-eyed poet named William
Wordsworth. Dazzled by the bright lights of "liberty,"
"equality," and "fraternity" for the French, Wordsworth
mooned in verse:

> Bliss was it in that dawn to be alive,
> But to be young was very heaven.

What followed in the next troubled years brought disen-
chantment and cynicism to which the young poet gave vent
in hot confession:

> I lost
> all feeling of conviction, and, in fine,
> Sick, wearied out with contrarieties,
> Yielded up moral questions in despair.

His commitment was as short-lived as it was hot-blooded.

Some of us have had short-term commitments whose vanishing has done little to enrich our memory and nothing at all to enhance our character. We have walked out on a spouse. We have let a friendship sicken and die. We have seen a vow go limp with compromise. We have watched a tither's pledge go down the drain of fabricated excuses. And just maybe, we have seen our vocation of preacher turn stealthily down the alley of lust and sleaze.

Commitment! Dear God, you have seen its collapse in our cheap accommodations to wrong. You have watched with pain and protest as the world's termites eat the once strong timbers out of our conscience and character.

Miriam Teichner fashioned a prayer that all of us might well make our own, if it is continuity of commitment that we seriously long to demonstrate:

> Give me the heart that divines, understands,
> Give me the courage, wounded, to fight.
> Flood me with knowledge, drench me with light,
> Please, keep me eager just to do my share.
> God—let me be aware.

Crises

Listening again to that voice of commitment from the cross, we are reminded that commitment has its crises no less certainly than it has its commencement and its continuity.

Look back on the unfolding life of Jesus. See the peaks and valleys in which his own dedication was tested and confirmed.

At age twelve, for example, Jesus faced a crisis of perception. He had gone along with his parents from Nazareth to

Jerusalem to observe the passover. Mary and Joseph started home for Nazareth in the company of their friends, unwittingly leaving Jesus behind. Returning to Jerusalem, they found him at last in the temple, where he was confounding the teachers with his insights. When Mary reproved him for not keeping step with the family, he had to tell them that he was beginning openly to march to a different drummer. He was precisely where he belonged, in his Father's "house" (NIV) doing his Father's "business" (KJV).

He was different, and they might as well know it now as later. His commitment to the Father's business was showing its hand. Faced with graded loyalties—to his earthly father Joseph and to his heavenly Father—he perceived the necessity of rating one above the other without repudiating either.

All of us come to such junctures in our lives. Sometimes the road forks, and the trick is to perceive which way is right and which way is wrong. Sometimes the choices are multiple, and the decision is between better and best.

> To every man there openeth
>   A highway and a low
> And every man decideth
>   Which way his soul shall go.
>
> The easy path of the lowland
>   Hath little of grand or new,
> While the toilsome ascent leads on
>   To a vast and glorious view.
>
> Peopled and warm the valley,
>   Lonely and chill the height;
> But the path that is nearest the storm cloud
>   Is nearest the stars of light.

At such an hour of crisis, long before death, it is splendidly appropriate to say discerningly, "Father, into your hands I commit my spirit."

Or, take the crisis of motivation that may be seen in that experience of Jesus that we call his transfiguration. Luke records it, vividly and memorably. Jesus is in the north country. It was probably on Mount Hermon that he suddenly became luminous with a splendor so entrancing that Peter, one of the eye-witnesses, wanted to make a shrine there and never leave it.

Wasn't this reason enough for Jesus to end his life-style as a peasant, reason enough for him to escape the daily barrage of tricky questions or the malicious agenda of fault finding, cleverly contrived by those who were determined to discredit him?

What relief! What comfort! What bliss! Just to stay where it was all like a rose garden in paradise! But Jesus rejected the idea. This was not the goal of his coming to live among men. He didn't come to spare himself. He came to give himself, let the cost be what it may.

So, with goal freshly in view and motivation newly clarified, he returned from the peak of splendor to the valley of pain and tears, of wracked bodies and tortured minds, of ugly guilts and fierce hates. It is no accident, therefore, that Jesus turned from the relative calm and safety of Galilee and "resolutely set out for Jerusalem" (Luke 9:51). After all, he hadn't come among us to prolong his life but to give it, to fulfill its purpose, to break the grip of our strangling self-centeredness, and to give to life—your life and mine—a brand-new pattern and purpose.

In Athens, long ago, that wandering genius Socrates said, "I do nothing but go about persuading you all, old and young alike, not to take thought for your persons or your property, but first and chiefly to care about the greatest improvement of the soul." What Socrates soundly discerned as a worthy motive for living, Christ both approves and fulfills.

Then there was the crisis of identification. The word seems bland enough, but seen in context it becomes radically exciting. We are in the Gethsemane garden now. Not the thought of dying but of dying *as a sinner* is so appalling to the sinless One that it prostrates him. He cannot repress the urge to ask, if possible, for a way out. His plea emerges from the incomparable mystery of his identity with the Father, on the one hand, and his identity with the Father's world of alienated human beings, on the other hand.

The agony, with its groans, punctures the silence of the night: "Father, if you are willing, take this cup from me; yet not my will, but yours be done" (Luke 22:42).

Mirrored here, for Christians, is the crisis of crises. For many Christians it comes early on in their walk with the Lord. For many it comes later.

I recall a saying of that remarkably committed Episcopal rector, "Sam" Shoemaker: "Sooner or later every Christian must face a choice between two pains, the pain of a divided mind or the pain of a crucified ego."

George Mueller, of world fame in Christian circles as a man extraordinarily at home in the realm of prayer and faith, said:

> There was a day when I died, utterly died, died to George Mueller, his opinions, preferences, tastes, and will—died to the world, its approval or censure—died to the approval or blame even of my brethren or friends—and since then I have studied only to show myself approved unto God.

If some doctrinal squeamishness holds you back from describing this as a "second blessing," so be it. But God forgive you, if your Christian commitment is one whit less than what George Mueller of Bristol gave to the Jesus of the cross.

Coronation

Think, finally, of commitment's coronation. Here, in our text, are deathless words from a dying Savior: "Father, into your hands I commit my spirit." Words that will forever live from One who, once dead, and risen, will never die again! But this is getting ahead of what Jesus said on the verge of his own death.

As we were reminded at the beginning, these words were David's in Psalm 31:5. David used them not when he was about to die but when he was confident of being spared in a near brush with death. The second half of Psalm 31:5 reads: "Redeem me, O LORD, the God of truth." I agree with Alexander Maclaren that "redeem" here means not redemption from sin in the New Testament sense, but rather to rescue a person from those who have set a trap for him.

In any case, our dying Lord, recalling these words, turns them first into a direct address to the Father, and then takes them to himself as being perfectly appropriate to the handing over of his spirit to the Father's keeping. Here was the supreme act of commitment, the climactic and total entrustment of himself into the hands of the God who is *over* all, and *in* all, and *through* all.

Never again would people hound him or hurt him. Never again would they bait him or bruise him. Never again would they curse him or crush him. Never again would they sting him with leer or jeer.

On the contrary, from his exalted station, which Scripture calls the Father's "right hand," he will offer to love them and lead them, help them and heal them, purify them and polish them, teach them and train them, gift them and govern them, ennoble them and enhance them until, some bright morning or some illumined midnight, they, too, shall commit themselves to the Father's endless keeping.

My own father, more than a half-century ago, in the act of dying, took the mystery of heaven and reduced it to an incredibly alluring simplicity. It was daybreak on a May morning. Through the long hours of the night I had watched him. He grew mildly restless. I bent over him. "Is there anything I can do, Father?" A short pause. My hand was around his as I bent over him.

"Paul," he whispered, "I'm almost home!"

He spoke no more.

Jesus, in the Father's hands, was a winner. So, too, I am convinced, was my father. So, too, you and I can be.